This series offers the concerned reader basic guidelines and *practical* applications of religion for today's world. Although decidedly Christian in focus and emphasis, the series embraces all denominations and modes of Bible-based belief relevant to our lives today. All volumes in the Steeple series are originals, freshly written to provide a fresh perspective on current—and yet timeless—human dilemmas. This is a series for our times.

Among the books:

*Woman in Despair: A Christian
Guide to Self-Repair*
Elizabeth Rice Handford

A Spiritual Handbook for Women
Dandi Daley Knorr

How to Read the Bible
James Fischer

*Bible Solutions to Problems
of Daily Living*
James W. Steele

*A Book of Devotions
for Today's Woman*
Frances Carroll

*Temptation: How Christians
Can Deal with It*
Frances Carroll

*With God on Your Side: A Guide
to Finding Self-Worth
Through Total Faith*
Doug Manning

*Help in Ages Past, Hope for Years
to Come: Daily Devotions
from the Old Testament*
Robert L. Cate

*Walking in the Garden: Inner Peace
from the Flowers of God*
Paula Connor

*How to Bring up Children
in the Catholic Faith*
Carol and David Powell

*A Daily Key for Today's Christians:
365 Key Texts
of the New Testament*
William E. Bowles

*How to Talk with God Every Day
of the Year: A Book of Devotions
for Twelve Positive Months*
Frances Hunter

*God's Conditions for Prosperity:
How to Earn the Rewards
of Christian Living*
Charles Hunter

*Pilgrimages: A Guide
to the Holy Places of Europe
for Today's Traveler*
Paul Lambourne Higgins

*Journey into the Light: Lessons
of Pain and Joy to Renew Your
Energy and Strengthen Your Faith*
Dorris Blough Murdock

Prentice-Hall International, Inc., *London*
Prentice-Hall of Australia Pty. Limited, *Sydney*
Prentice-Hall Canada Inc., *Toronto*
Prentice-Hall of India Private Limited, *New Delhi*
Prentice-Hall of Japan, Inc., *Tokyo*
Prentice-Hall of Southeast Asia Pte. Ltd., *Singapore*
Whitehall Books Limited, *Wellington, New Zealand*
Editora Prentice-Hall do Brasil Ltda., *Rio de Janeiro*

Michael R. Cosby
Sex in the Bible
An Introduction to What the Scriptures Teach Us About Sexuality

105436

A SPECTRUM BOOK

Prentice-Hall, Inc., Englewood Cliffs, New Jersey 07632

Library of Congress Cataloging in Publication Data

Cosby, Michael R.
   Sex in the Bible.

   (Steeple books)
   "A Spectrum Book."
   Includes index.
   1. Sex—Biblical teaching.   I. Title.   II. Series.
   BS680.S5C66   1984   241'.66   83-16090
   ISBN 0-13-807280-9
   ISBN 0-13-807272-8 (pbk.)

To Lynne

© 1984 by Prentice-Hall, Inc., Englewood Cliffs, New Jersey 07632.
All rights reserved. No part of this book may be reproduced in any form
or by any means without permission in writing from the publisher.
A Spectrum Book. Printed in the United States of America.

1   2   3   4   5   6   7   8   9   10

ISBN 0-13-807280-9

ISBN 0-13-807272-8 {PBK.}

Editorial/production supervision
and interior calligraphy by Chris McMorrow
Cover design by Hal Siegel
Manufacturing buyer: Edward J. Ellis

This book is available at a special discount when ordered in
bulk quantities. Contact Prentice-Hall, Inc., General
Publishing Division, Special Sales, Englewood Cliffs, N.J. 07632.

Contents

Preface   vii

1

Biblical Sexuality from a Modern Perspective 1

2

Deuteronomy: Theological Foundations for Sex 7

3

Proverbs: a Rational Approach for Sexual Morality 29

4

Song of Songs: a Celebration of the Sensuous 53

5

*The Gospels: Jesus' Teaching
on Radical Love and Moral Purity*   83

6

*1 Corinthians: Apostolic Correction
of Sexual Aberration*   103

7

*Romans 1:18–32: Homosexuality in Antiquity
and Paul's Argument from Natural Order*   141

8

Modern Sexuality and Biblical Perspectives   167

Index   179

Preface

Reading what various books of the Bible say about matters such as sex, marriage, divorce, and homosexuality can be a rather confusing experience, even for those who fancy that they know a good deal about the Bible. The cultures in which the biblical authors lived were so vastly different from our own that it is possible to perceive clearly enough *what* a passage says about a particular issue but still be mystified concerning the reason *why* it was written. This book is designed to help you understand both the *what* and the *why* of biblical statements on sexuality, whether you are at home in the Bible or are a novice to its contents.

Since the Bible contains a large number of books written over a time span of centuries in a variety of different social and political settings, determining how to approach its contents can be formidable. Some approach is needed to simplify the study and make the relevant biblical material accessible without treating it simplistically. The approach taken in this book is to examine a limited number of biblical texts that are representative of the content found when reading on a wider scale. Instead of looking superficially at a large number of texts, this study provides a more in-depth study of a set of carefully selected documents.

To understand what any one biblical author wrote about matters pertaining to sex, it is important to comprehend something about the culture in which that individual lived. This is, perhaps, rather obvious. But there is another important factor that people often tend to overlook: the overall scope of the work in which a statement about sex is made. To understand the meaning of any one statement in a book, it is frequently very important to interpret it in light of the author's overall purpose in the document as a whole. Therefore, this investigation seeks to explain the cultural settings of various biblical authors and also to elucidate how their statements on sexuality find meaning in the larger scope of their individual works. This two-dimensional approach will enhance your ability to have a dialogue with the biblical material and to sharpen your thinking on the ideal role of sex in your own society and in your own life.

Sexual dimensions of human relationships can produce tremendous joy, but they can also be part of terrible misery through distorted and broken relationships. Careful reflection upon how to be successful in life, experiencing joy instead of misery, can benefit tremendously from entering into dialogue with the biblical authors. Although Western culture has undergone and is undergoing a sexual revolution, the Bible continues to play a significant role in the shaping of ethical and moral standards. Therefore the study of what is said about sex in Scripture is of importance not only for those who seek to define their moral stance by the Bible but also for those who give it no special place of authority in their lives. Intelligent reflection on issues such as marriage, divorce, extramarital sex, premarital sex, and homosexuality is enhanced by understanding what the biblical authors said about these matters and the underlying reasons for their statements. Your thinking will almost certainly be modified in some way as a result of reading this book.

I would like to thank the following people for reading parts of the manuscript and offering valuable constructive criticism: William Beardslee, Fred Craddock, John Gammie, Hoy and Jary Ledbetter, Pat Nave, Carol Newsom, and Gene Tucker. Special thanks go to Arthur Wainwright for his encouragement and advice all through the writing

of this book. Most of all I thank my wife, Lynne, who unselfishly devoted numerous weekends to typing each of the chapters, after carefully reading and editing them and offering many valuable suggestions.

Acknowledgments

Old Testament and Apocrypha quotations are from the Revised Standard Version of the Bible, copyrighted 1946, 1952 © 1971, 1973, and are used by permission. (New Testament quotations are the author's own translations.) Oxford University Press graciously granted permission for the quotations used from the Pseudepigrapha and the Mishnah. Harvard University Press kindly gave permission for use of the numerous quotations from the Loeb Classical Library. Penguin Books Ltd. allowed the use of a quotation from Green's translation of Juvenal's *Sixth Satire* and Guthrie's translation of Plato's *Protagorus*.

Biblical Sexuality from a Modern Perspective

1

> If a man meets a virgin who is not betrothed, and seizes her and lies with her, and they are found, then the man who lay with her shall give to the father of the young woman fifty shekels of silver, and she shall be his wife, because he has violated her; he may not put her away all his days.
>
> *(Deuteronomy 22:28–29)*

Can you imagine a law such as this being implemented today in a court case involving rape? Try to picture a judge looking sternly over the top of his glasses, which have slid down slightly upon his nose, at a nervous young man standing before his desk. Over to one side sits a young woman showing obvious signs of stress, the victim of a frightening and traumatic experience. Close to her is her family, tight-lipped and bitter. All attention is riveted on the judge, who ominously clears his throat and reads the sentence: "The verdict of this court is that you are guilty of raping this young woman. Therefore, you must pay her father the standard bride price of fifty shekels of silver and take her in marriage. Furthermore, because you have humiliated her by your dreadful behavior, you have forfeited your normal right to divorce. Until you die you must keep her as your wife."

Perhaps your initial reaction to this law from Deuteronomy is one of amazed disbelief or even outrage. Why would anyone write legislation prescribing indissoluble marriage between a rapist and his victim? Is this not a cruel and heartless thing to force upon a young woman? From our own cultural perspective such a law would seem to be a terrible perversion of justice, so we may well wonder why ancient Hebrew society considered it to be just. Admittedly this example appears somewhat extreme, and we will see in Chapter 2 on Deuteronomy that Hebrew society did not apply such legislation in every case. Yet as we progress through our study of sex in the Bible, we will encounter other statements that initially sound equally strange. This should come as no surprise. The ancient cultures in which the biblical documents were written were so different from our own that many of their customs are bound to strike us as very odd.

Understanding what is said in the Bible about matters such as sex, marriage, divorce, and homosexuality can be like going on a jungle safari if you have never ventured far from a home in the city. You need a guide. The terrain is unfamiliar, and the language and customs of the jungle dwellers are vastly different from your own. Your guide may interpret for you what the people are saying, but the meaning of their words will probably remain puzzling unless he also explains something about the beliefs and customs of the people. You are so accustomed to thinking in terms of Western cultural standards that you might easily misinterpret what people say due to the tendency to impose your own cultural concepts upon their words. Imagine the misunderstanding involved in a conversation with a polygamous tribal chief on the topic of marriage if you are interpreting what he is saying in light of your own monogamous society! Although you may think that you have understood his words, you may be far from actually hearing what he means when he speaks those same words. So it is with the Bible.

Unless you know something about the cultures in which the biblical authors lived and wrote, you may well be familiar with their words but a foreigner to their meaning. Ideally, this realization of the oddness or unfamilarity of many biblical statements should stimulate

our curiosity, creating a desire to understand why the ancient Hebrews held these viewpoints on rape and other sensitive matters. To be content to ask only *what* a biblical passage says is to remain on a superficial level that keeps us from understanding the true intent of that material. When we begin to probe to a deeper level, however, by asking *why*, we become more aware of the fact that the authors of the Bible were wrestling with many of the same problems we face today. For example, during recent years our culture has seen considerable modification of traditional values in sexual morality. What is commonplace today would have been utterly shocking not too many years ago. Yet we should not think that this situation is unique in history. Some of the biblical authors addressed similar conditions, and the study of their responses, as well as of the alternatives they proposed, has a perennial relevance. Thus, when we expend the effort necessary to penetrate through the initially peculiar sound of what they said, we discover that, although they lived in cultural settings very foreign to us, they addressed many issues that are truly contemporary.

To benefit fully from the writings of the biblical authors, we must seriously consider the fact that these people did not write in a historical vacuum. The books that were collected to form the Bible were written over a time span of centuries in a number of different political situations by individuals occupying various levels of society. Some were relatively wealthy; some were poor. Some defended the status quo; others spoke forcefully against corrupt government. Over the centuries during which they wrote there were good and bad governments, times of economic prosperity and times of famine, eras of national independence and a great amount of subjection to foreign powers. The biblical documents represent a wide variety of responses to very real historical situations. Regardless of whether the biblical authors wrote historical accounts or poetry or prophetic proclamations or personal letters, they wrote for specific purposes. Therefore, if we are to understand what any book of the Bible says about sexuality, we must do so in light of the author's larger purpose in writing.

With this in mind, we will limit the scope of our investigation to significant material in a few biblical books, material that is representa-

tive of the content we would find if we were to read more broadly. We will not attempt to answer a question like, What does the Bible say about sex? The very way in which such a question is worded seems to assume that all of the biblical books present one simple point of view, as if the great differences in time and purpose between the books were insignificant. This is totally unrealistic. On the one hand there is considerable unity in what the authors of the Bible said about sexual morality. But on the other hand, as we examine each individual writing, we will see that there is also progression of thought, in matters pertaining to divorce, for example. Our task, therefore, will be to trace both the unity and the diversity, observing not only how thinking on various issues changed but also asking why it changed. As a result of interacting with the biblical material in this way, we will be better able to reflect upon our own contemporary situations.

Our study will devote three chapters to three different books of the Old Testament, as well as three chapters to two important New Testament figures, Jesus and Paul. As we progress through the legislated morality of Deuteronomy, to the educationally oriented approach of the Hebrew Wisdom School as represented in Proverbs, and on to the delightfully explicit love poetry of the Song of Songs, we will encounter both open appreciation of sexual enjoyment within marriage and extreme harshness toward sexual offenders. With Jesus some of the older attitudes toward marriage and divorce are severely challenged, while the overall moral code is largely affirmed. Finally, the Apostle Paul, with his driving missionary zeal and expectation of the cataclysmic end of the world, provides his own very intriguing ideas on marriage in particular. Each book or individual presents a unique viewpoint, presenting us with a vision of reality that has great potential in the shaping of our own thought. As we launch our investigation, therefore, we may do so with a sense of expectancy, for both the topic of study and the biblical material are extremely important in their own rights.

Deuteronomy: Theological Foundations for Sex

2

Ancient Hebrew Culture
in Perspective

Our study begins with Deuteronomy, a book that provides important foundational material for understanding the development of biblical sexuality. The information, however, is primarily in the form of a law code—specific rules governing virtually every aspect of ancient Israelite life. Deuteronomy contains legislation on everything from directions for waging war (for example, Deut. 20) to a regulation on the correct procedure for taking eggs from a bird's nest (22:6–7). Scattered among these diverse laws are commands concerning the sexual life of the people, commands that, from a modern perspective, often sound very strange indeed.

Since the ancient culture for which the laws of Deuteronomy were written was vastly different from our own, do not be surprised if you are shocked when you read some of them. Remember that the study of any foreign culture requires sensitive effort in order to understand and appreciate the underlying reasons for the existence of what appear to be rather odd customs. You may find it very difficult to see the world

through ancient Hebrew eyes, and you might be offended by their view of women or their understanding of marriage. In spite of the fact that many of the sexual laws in Deuteronomy may seem strange, they actually reveal a close connection to the kinds of issues that many religious people encounter today, since the Hebrews also faced the problem of living in the midst of cultures that promoted views on sex differing from their own.

When we see that this ancient Hebrew society struggled to maintain a sexual ethic that had both much in common with its neighbors and also much in conflict, it is easier to empathize with their situation. How much shall the community's moral standards conform to the broader cultural context, and how much should they stand against the general trends? These questions have a perennial relevance and have been answered in a variety of ways during the long history of Judaism and Christianity.

In order to understand the sexual norms of Deuteronomy, it is important to recognize that the author understood the Hebrew people as a society under the rule of God.[1] He saw the laws in Deuteronomy as God's laws, not merely human legislation. To attempt to see reality through the eyes of this ancient author, it is necessary to understand the way in which his book is built on the notion of covenant. The narrative sections that precede and follow the lengthy list of laws in chapters 12–26 are largely devoted to explaining how God's covenant with the Hebrew people provides the basis for obedience to this legislation. They were to follow the rules because they had entered into a contract or signed a treaty with God—a contract that specified what both God and the people were responsible to do, a treaty between God and the Hebrews built upon a format familiar to peoples of the Ancient Near East.

It was a common practice for a conquering nation to make treaties with less powerful states that had surrendered to it. The ruling nation would write a covenant document stipulating what the subjugated state could and could not do, and in return for compliance with these stipulations the dominant power provided military protection. These documents often included both some sort of historical account of the

events leading up to and including the writing of the covenant and a section of warnings stipulating what terrible retaliatory measures would be taken against the subjugated state if it rebelled and broke the covenant. The similarity between this ancient covenant format and the way in which Deuteronomy is written is striking.

The book begins with an account of Moses reminding the Israelites of how they had entered into a sworn covenant with Yahweh,[2] their God, some forty years earlier at Mount Horeb, where Yahweh gave them the Ten Commandments; how, by their disobedience to God, they had been denied entry into the promised land at that time; and how for forty years they had wandered through the wilderness. Now, on this momentous day, they are to renew their covenant with Yahweh. Moses stresses and restresses the importance of obedience to the stipulations of this covenant; and, in a lengthy manner, he recites for them these stipulations: As the covenant people of God they must remain absolutely loyal to Yahweh and his commands, shunning the religious practices of the surrounding peoples. He reminds the Israelites that if they obey God, they will experience only his blessings, enjoying such things as good health, safety from their enemies, the births of many children, and productive animals and land; but if they break the covenant by committing apostasy, he warns in terrifying threats that they will experience the opposite of the good life, suffering destruction from their enemies, blight on their land, barren wives, and barren animals. Thus in 11:26–28, Moses says,

> Behold, I set before you this day a blessing and a curse: the blessing, if you obey the commandments of the LORD your God, which I have commanded you this day, and the curse, if you do not obey the commandments of the LORD your God, but turn aside from the way which I command you this day, to go after other gods which you have not known.

On this day two roads lie before them: fullness of life and abundant blessing if they keep the covenant and a wretched life of destruction if they fail to keep it.

Sexuality in Deuteronomy must be understood in this covenant

context. Commands concerning sex were part of the total life-style of those who would experience the good life. To live by these norms was to enjoy what was, from the author's viewpoint, the ideal society. If the sexual stipulations were obeyed, God would give his blessing, but if broken, misery would result. Law codes of this type usually define what is considered to be incorrect behavior and explain what actions are to be followed if deviations occur, so it is understandable that Deuteronomy's laws deal more with correcting problems than they do with defining proper behavior. Nevertheless, careful study of these laws does enable us to see what was considered to be the proper expression of sexual behavior, as well as those actions thought to be deviant.

Marriage Relationships

Deuteronomy was written within a society that was decidedly male oriented, as were most ancient cultures. Reflecting the norms of a male-dominated society, the book takes for granted the belief that the wife is, to a certain degree, the property of the husband. The Hebrew term for husband, *ba'al* (see 24:4), means "lord"; and, following a marriage, the woman appears to have come under the rule of her husband. Though this does not imply that the husband had the right to treat his wife as a slave, it is clear that mention is only made of the husband divorcing the wife and never vice versa (21:14; 22:19, 29; 24:1–4) and of the husband seeking to verify his new bride's virginity but not vice versa (22:13–28). Although the woman was a responsible member of the covenant community in that if she broke the covenant and turned away to serve other gods, she was, like a man, to receive the same punishment of death by stoning (13:6–11; 17:2–7; 29:18–28), she nevertheless occupied a secondary position in society. Furthermore, loyalty to her husband, her *ba'al*, was strictly demanded.

In Deuteronomy sexual intercourse appears to be confined to the marriage relationship, forming a fidelity between husband and wife that, in some ways, reflects the covenant fidelity between God and his people Israel. Although the virginity of the man is never mentioned, it

is reasonable to assume, in light of the sexual restrictions placed upon the women, that in Deuteronomy's ideal society the man's sexual activity would also occur only within the confines of marriage. It is evident from 22:13–21 that the woman, at least, on pain of death, was to be a virgin until she married.

These strict confines, however, in no way indicate a devaluation of sexual relations. To promote joy in the marriage relationship, and to increase the likelihood of the birth of a son to continue the name of the husband in Israel, the man was exempt from military duties or from business obligations that would take him away from his new wife for the first year of marriage (20:7; 24:5). Explicitly, this law states that the husband was to be free to be at home so that he could "cause his wife to rejoice."[3] Thus, there was to be joy in the total relationship on the part of *both* male and female. In addition, God's blessing on the marriage would be seen in the production of children (6:3; 7:13–14; 28:4, 11; 30:9). So highly prized was the birth of children that their absence was considered part of the curses incurred for breach of the covenant (28:15–18). Obviously, the author of Deuteronomy had no need to ponder the ethics of birth control. Lower population density, higher infant mortality rates, and the advantages of having children to help in tilling the land combined to eliminate birth control as an issue of concern. Another factor is probably involved here, however, that goes beyond the advantages, in this ancient agricultural society, of having many children. Since there was no clearly developed concept of an afterlife in early Hebrew conceptualizations, a man was, to a certain degree, thought to live on in his sons.[4] It is, therefore, quite understandable why the production of a male heir was so important. This concern is given vivid expression in the law of levirate marriage, a provision made for the unfortunate situation of a man who dies with no male heir (25:5–10).

The levirate law stipulates that when two brothers live together, probably in a large family unit with shared responsibilities, and one dies without a son, the surviving brother is to take his brother's widow as a wife and have children by her so that the dead man's name may continue to live on in a son. You may well imagine how much of a

strain such an arrangement could place upon the surviving brother. He could be forced to acquire a wife he did not want; and if he were already married, he and his wife would have to adjust to the reality of having another woman inserted into their marriage relationship. And the widow of the dead brother also had no choice in the matter. She could be subjected to the humiliating circumstances involved in being an unwanted addition, or she might not find her new husband to be desirable.

The rather pathetic possibilities for pain in the levirate marriage may be glimpsed in the brief account of sordid events in Genesis 38. Nevertheless, in an ancient culture where a woman largely understood her role to be that of a provider of children for her husband, and where marriages were arranged by the parents, the dynamics involved in a levirate marriage were vastly different than if such a system were employed in our culture. There was a very strong societal pressure placed upon the surviving brother to keep his dead brother's name from being "blotted out of Israel" (25:6). If he refused to marry the widow, she was to have him brought before the elders of the city, where she would publicly humiliate him by spitting in his face; and he was to be branded by society as "the man who does not build up his brother's house" (25:9).

Polygamy and Interracial Marriage

Deuteronomy considers polygamy an acceptable practice, offering neither encouragement nor condemnation for it. In fact, having more than one wife would actually be expected in the case of levirate marriage if the surviving brother were already married. Polygamy might also be envisioned in two laws that are found in the context of regulations concerning the conquering of cities *outside* the promised land (20:14; 21:10–14). These commands allowed a soldier to take home a captive woman whom he considered to be beautiful and whom he desired to have for a wife (she had no choice in the matter). The only

requirement for such a marriage was that the soldier must have the woman shave her head, cut off her fingernails, put off her captive's garb, and mourn for her parents for one month[5] before he could consummate the marriage with sexual intercourse (21:13). It is quite probable that these requirements represent guidelines for purifying and assimilating the foreign wife into Hebrew society. In effect, she was to forsake the customs of her people and begin the practices of the Hebrews. Evidence for this may be seen in 14:1–2, a law regulating the way one is allowed to cut one's hair as a sign of mourning.

> You are the sons of the LORD your God; you shall not cut yourselves or make any baldness on your foreheads for the dead. For you are a people holy to the LORD your God, and the LORD has chosen you to be a people for his own possession, out of all the peoples that are on the face of the earth.

This law indicates that the Hebrews understood a distinction between their own custom of cutting the hair while mourning and similar mourning practices among the surrounding peoples—practices interwoven with their religious beliefs that were at variance with the Israelite covenant with Yahweh.[6] Thus, in the Canaanite Ras Shamra texts, there occurs this description: "The mourner . . . sat on the ground . . . wallowed in the dust and sprinkled it on his head, [and] lacerated his face with his nails. . . ."[7] Since facial laceration was part of the mourning practices of the Canaanites and other peoples, the stipulation in 21:12–13 that the captive woman must cut her nails is best understood as part of the process whereby she became part of the covenant community of Israel. She was allowed to mourn for her parents, but only in a way that was in keeping with Hebrew practice, not in the manner she had learned from her own culture. Thus, she must cut her hair for mourning in a Hebrew fashion and trim her nails so that she might not use them to lacerate her face in the custom of those who worship other gods. There is, therefore, no intended ban on interracial marriage—only a ban on the foreign wife's retention of former religious practices.[8]

Actually, Numbers 12:1–16 records an interesting story that

seems to attribute interracial marriage to none other than Moses himself. Moses, after marrying a "Cushite" woman, is criticized for his action by Miriam and Aaron; and, according to the story, God comes to Moses' defense and punishes Miriam for her unjust criticism. The land of Cush, also called Ethiopia, was located south of Egypt and was inhabited by very dark-skinned people. Jeremiah 13:23 actually records a proverb that asks, "Can the Ethiopian [Hebrew, "Cushite"] change his skin or the leopard his spots?" Although it is sometimes argued that "Cushite" in Numbers 12:1 could refer to people living in northern Arabia, and therefore merely be an obscure reference to Moses' Midianite wife, Zipporah, evidence for such a viewpoint is scarce. Admittedly, there are two problems with interpreting "Cushite" in Numbers 12:1 as an Ethiopian: (1) there is confusion over the identity of Moses' father-in-law (cf. Exodus 2:15–22; 18:1–27; and Numbers 10:29–31), who is once called a "Kenite" (Judges 4:11), a title designating a "metal smith"; and (2) if Moses' wife in Numbers 12:1 is not Zipporah, then she is mentioned nowhere else in the Old Testament. But the weight of evidence favors the meaning "Ethiopian" for the Hebrew "Cushite" in Numbers 12:1.

The story preserved in Numbers 12 implies that Moses had recently married the Cushite woman, and this fact was used by Aaron and Miriam to criticize him. Such details would be meaningless if applied to Zipporah. Furthermore, by far the most dominant meaning for "Cushite" in the Old Testament is "Ethiopian," a fact that is clearly illustrated in the Septuagint, the Greek translation made of the Old Testament beginning in the third century B.C. Except for 2 Samuel 18:21–23, 31–32, where the Septuagint merely transliterates the Hebrew "Cushite" into a Greek word with a similar vocalization, the Septuagint always translates "Cushite" as "Ethiopian"; and this holds true for Numbers 12:1. So, although we are given no details about the marriage in this brief reference, it appears that the story reports that Moses, the great lawgiver of Deuteronomy, married a black woman.

Problems clearly are foreseen in Deuteronomy in the context of interracial marriage, yet these difficulties center on issues arising when a man and woman from different cultural backgrounds attempt to

adapt to each other's ways. For that time as well as for today, cultural and religious differences can place great stress on a marriage relationship. One law in Deuteronomy regulates the activities of the Israelite king by commanding, "He shall not multiply wives for himself, lest his heart turn away" (17:17). Probably the best example of this actually happening occurs in 1 Kings 11:1–8:

> Now King Solomon loved many foreign women . . . from the nations concerning which the LORD had said to the people of Israel, "You shall not enter into marriage with them, . . . for surely they will turn away your heart after their gods." . . . When Solomon was old his wives turned away his heart after other gods; and his heart was not wholly true to the LORD his God. . . .

This temptation to apostasy due to the influence of foreign wives was not limited to the king, however, as may be seen in Deuteronomy 7:3. This command is located in a description of how to conduct warfare against the peoples *within* the promised land and concerns Hebrew soldiers. Whereas in warfare against cities outside the promised land, soldiers could take prisoners, the Israelites were ordered to destroy the entire populations of the cities they conquered within the land. They were not allowed to spare them or to make treaties/covenants with them. The Hebrew term used here, *berît*, is the same one used elsewhere to describe Israel's covenant with God. Israel had made a covenant with God, and no covenants were to be made with the surrounding nations, for that would violate the treaty with God.

Often in the Ancient Near East, covenants/treaties were solidified by marriage alliances (for example, the king of one country might take a daughter of another king as one of his wives), and the marriage prohibition of 7:3 should be seen in this light. Note the sequence of 7:2–4: ". . . you must utterly destroy them; you shall make no covenant with them. . . . You shall not make marriages with them . . . for they would turn away your sons from following me, to serve other gods." So although it was permissible for a soldier to bring back a foreign wife and assimilate her into Hebrew culture, it was not permissible for a king to enter into a covenant with another state by marrying

(or having his son marry) a royal representative of that foreign government. By virtue of the treaty, such women would have to be allowed to maintain their former religious practices. Marriage alliances and their resulting influences toward apostasy were therefore forbidden in order to maintain covenant loyalty to Yahweh. It is apostasy, not polygamy or foreign marriages in themselves, that is at issue. Israel must preserve loyalty to God.

Although polygamy is perfectly acceptable in the society proposed by Deuteronomy, difficulties arising from polygamous marriages are recognized. For example, if the husband loves one of his wives a lot more than the other(s), intense problems might arise due to the favoritism he might show to her and her children. A good illustration of this may be seen in Genesis 29:15–30:24. This is a story filled with pathos, describing the great pain experienced by Leah because Jacob loved his other wife, Rachel, much more. Leah repeatedly sought to gain Jacob's favor by bearing children for him, but she was never able to win his love. Jacob's favoritism also caused interfamily conflict among his children, for Leah's sons resented the favored status of Rachel's sons. In an attempt to regulate such problems, the law in Deut. 21:15–17 specifies that the firstborn's right of inheritance, namely twice what the other sons receive, could not be denied the first son of the unloved wife if he were born before the first son of the wife whom the husband loved. Interestingly, although this law forbids any attempt to set aside the right of the firstborn son, it is completely silent concerning the plight of the unloved wife. In reality, however, the majority of Hebrew men were not financially able to maintain more than one wife anyway, so polygamy, though acceptable, was not prevalent.

Divorce

A man was under no compulsion to retain a wife whom he did not want. In keeping with the male-dominated society, Deuteronomy considers divorce to be the right of the man, but never mentions it as a

possibility for the woman. If it was permissible for a woman to divorce her husband, Deuteronomy is silent concerning the matter. Although divorce is nowhere commanded in the book, the right for the male to divorce his wife if he so chooses is clear from two passages. The first instance is in 21:10–14, the law mentioned previously that concerns a soldier bringing home a female captive of war. After taking her for his wife, he may divorce her if he finds no delight in her, but may not sell her as a slave, probably because of her forced assimilation into the community of Israel prior to the consummation of the marriage. The second instance is in 24:1–4, a law that applies to divorcing women of Hebrew descent as well as foreign wives. Since this passage forms the basis for an argument between Jesus and some Pharisees in Mark 10:2–10 and Matthew 19:3–9 over the legitimacy of divorce, it has received considerable attention from Christians. Unfortunately, many people fail to recognize that this law does not legislate legitimate reasons for divorce, but merely prohibits a situation that may arise as a result of divorce.

> [1]When a man takes a wife and marries her, if then she finds no favor in his eyes because he has found some indecency in her, and he writes her a bill of divorce and puts it in her hand and sends her out of his house, and she departs out of his house, [2]and if she goes and becomes another man's wife, [3]and the latter husband dislikes her and writes her a bill of divorce and puts it in her hand and sends her out of his house, or if the latter husband dies, who took her to be his wife, [4]then her former husband, who sent her away, may not take her again to be his wife, after she has been defiled; for that is an abomination before the LORD, and you shall not bring guilt upon the land which the LORD your God gives you for an inheritance.

Notice that the law is written in a stylized form that is very common in Deuteronomy 12–26: "*If* _____ event occurs or _____ situation exists, *then* you shall (or shall not) do the following." Only if the initial conditions are true does the law come into effect. Thus, 24:1–3 merely defines the circumstances that must be true in order for the regulation of remarriage in 24:4 to come into effect. Divorce is simply assumed by the law. If a man decided to divorce his wife, he placed a

divorce document in her hand and formally ejected her from his house. This document, which needed the signatures of several witnesses, usually contained three elements:

1. A statement of release saying that the woman was no longer his wife
2. Permission for her to remarry
3. Identification of the letter as a divorce document

Since sexual intercourse with another man's wife carried the death penalty, this divorce document was important verification that the woman was available for remarriage.

Interpreting 24:1–4 is extremely difficult, because this law apparently assumes that its ancient readers understood considerably more about the reasons for its prohibition than is presently possible for the modern reader. For example, the phrase translated "some indecency" in verse 1 (Hebrew, *'erwat dābār*) literally means some "matter of nakedness"; and, depending on the context, "nakedness" (*'erwat*) can be used to designate a variety of things. In this particular situation it appears to indicate some sort of shameful action or condition and may be intentionally broad in scope, allowing for any number of possible situations. Apparently it does not refer to adultery, since death, not divorce, is prescribed for adultery in 22:22, 23–24. Verses 2–3 are even less defined than verse 1, giving as a reason for divorce only that the second husband does not like the woman (however, verse 3b allows for the possibility that the second husband might be satisfied enough with the woman that she remained his wife until his death). Although verse 4 clearly forbids the first husband to remarry his former wife after she has been married to another, the only explanation given for this prohibition is that such marriage is so profane that it would defile the land.

The land was considered to be, if not *the* most important, one of the most important gifts of God to the Hebrew people as a result of his covenant with them. And the ancient Israelites did not view the land as most people do today, merely as weathered rock containing various kinds of organic matter. For them the soil had some sort of mysterious identity as a living entity, and it was their duty to keep the land pure even as

they would try to maintain their personal purity. Indeed, if the land was polluted in some way, they were to perform rituals designed to restore its purity—rituals not that dissimilar from those conducted to purify people.[9] When the land was polluted, it was an extremely serious matter which had to be corrected, for all of the people might suffer as a result—not just the ones committing the offense. Therefore the warning in 24:4 is very important, although the reason why such remarriage defiles the land is obscure.

Since marriage to a third husband would be considered legitimate in ancient Hebrew society, it appears that this law is only concerned to ban remarriage after an intervening marriage.[10] On the one hand, 24:1–4 reveals a belief in the extremely serious nature of such a remarriage; but, on the other hand, it provides little aid in understanding why the Hebrews considered such an action to be so grave. Evidence from Jeremiah 3:1 indicates that people apparently understood the reason and therefore no explanation was needed, for the prophet says, "If a man divorces his wife and she goes from him and becomes another man's wife, will he return to her? Would not the land be greatly polluted?" Scholars have made a number of conjectures as to the reasons underlying Deut. 24:1–4, but none of them is particularly convincing. Legislating against a certain type of remarriage and speaking only indirectly to the problem of divorce, the rationale for the law appears to be lost in antiquity.

Premarital Sex, Adultery, and Rape

In Deuteronomy divorce is forbidden in only two situations: when a man has falsely accused his new wife of not being a virgin when he married her (22:13–19) and when a man rapes a virgin and is consequently forced to marry her (22:28–29). Both of these instances are cases in which the man has unlawfully abused the woman and as a result forfeits his right to divorce her. In neither case is the possibility even mentioned that the wife might divorce the man.

The first instance (22:13–19) involves a situation where, shortly after a marriage is consummated, the husband goes to his father-in-law and states that he did not find in his new wife the "tokens of virginity." As in the previous example on divorce (24:1–4), some aspects of this law are not totally clear. Most likely "tokens of virginity" refers to the bloodstains on the bedcover resulting from sexual intercourse on the wedding night.[11] The husband's accusation was no small matter; for if his charge were true, his wife was to be killed by stoning at the door of her father's house, "because she has wrought folly in Israel by playing the harlot in her father's house" (22:21). By making his charge, the husband would bring public disgrace upon his wife and her parents. Consequently, the woman's parents were obliged to produce the bloodstained bedcover as evidence to the elders of the city, who acted as judges in such matters, that their daughter was a virgin when they delivered her to the man.

An obvious difficulty with interpreting "tokens of virginity" as nuptial bloodstains is that it is hard to imagine why the husband would have been ignorant of their presence, especially in light of the severe consequence for himself or his bride. If the parents of the bride produced the evidence, the elders were to have the new husband who had made this false accusation beaten publicly and fined 100 pieces of silver to be awarded to the bride's father. Since the average bride price was 50 pieces of silver (22:29), the brash husband was actually to have been fined twice the bride price, which was over and above the price he had already paid for the woman. Because this heavy fine was paid to the bride's father, or, if the woman were guilty, her death was to be at her father's door, this law indicates that the greatest indignity was seen to have been suffered by the father. To have a betrothed, nonvirgin daughter was a disgrace to the father, who was evidently responsible for seeing that such a thing did not happen.

Although it is perhaps difficult for people in Western societies to understand the extreme value that the ancient Hebrews placed on premarital virginity, many who live in Near Eastern cultures would be much more aware of this value system. S. R. Driver's commentary on Deuteronomy provides illustrative information from various Bedouin

and rural societies.[12] For example, among some Arabs in Egypt and some village people in Syria and Palestine, the proud parents of the virgin bride would exhibit the bloodstained wedding-night bedcloth to relations or even hang it out for public display to the neighbors. Such customs may be somewhat shocking to us today, but they help to illustrate the value placed upon premarital virginity in Deuteronomy. A woman's value as her husband's prized possession would be reduced if she were not a virgin bride. We should also keep in mind that since the man was thought to live on through his children, it was of vital importance that his wife's offspring be legitimate.

The second law in Deuteronomy forbidding divorce (22:28–29) envisions a situation in which a man rapes an unbetrothed virgin and is caught in the act. Since she does not belong to another man, the ravisher is obliged to pay the bride price of fifty pieces of silver to her father and to marry her.[13] If the girl has been betrothed to another man, however, the rapist is to be killed (22:25–27).[14] Betrothal was a binding, legal contract that could be dissolved only by divorce in ancient Israel. From the viewpoint of the law, therefore, rape was not merely an offense against a woman. If a man raped another man's wife, he had violated the possession of another man and had to die. If he raped an unbetrothed girl, he was forced to have a permanent wife, presumably as a protective measure to ensure that the girl, and any possible child, would be provided for by the guilty party. Since the woman's value would be diminished if she lost her virginity, and other eligible men might therefore not want to marry her, precautions were taken to ensure that she would be supported. Because there is no mention of the double suffering inflicted upon the victimized woman, who is forced to marry the very man who raped her, it would be good to point out that these laws sometimes do not tell the whole story. For example, the parallel law in Exodus 22:16–17 allows the girl's father to refuse to give her in marriage to the rapist.

Adultery, a sexual deviation also punishable by death, is forbidden in 5:18 and 21 and may pertain either to sexual intercourse with another man's wife (22:22) or to sex with another man's betrothed virgin (22:23–24), who, unlike the girl who was raped in 22:25, is a

willing accomplice.[15] In either case, both the man and his female accomplice are stoned to death at the gate of the city. Death, not divorce, was the penalty for those caught in adultery. The covenant community of Israel was not to allow sexual infidelity.

Prostitution, Transvestism, and Incest

There are two kinds of prostitution mentioned in Deuteronomy, and both are forbidden. The first is the typical "sex for money" variety and is labeled as an abomination to the LORD (23:18). The second type is cultic prostitution, a common form of religious ritual practiced by some of Israel's neighboring societies (23:17). In the Hebrew language a regular prostitute was called a *zônâ*, and a cultic prostitute was called a *qed̄ēśâ*. The title *qed̄ēśâ* reveals an interesting bit of information about the viewpoint of Israel's neighbors concerning cultic prostitution, for the Hebrew term used to describe "holiness" or "sacredness" was *qōd̄ēś*, the root for *qed̄ēśâ*. These neighboring cultures considered cult prostitutes to be "set apart" or "dedicated" to the service of particular gods, and their title literally means "holy ones." Both men and women served as cult prostitutes in these religious sexual observances, and participation in such cultic rituals to other gods was absolutely forbidden for Israel's covenant members. Thus 23:17 reads, "There shall be no cult prostitute (*qed̄ēśâ*) of the daughters of Israel, neither shall there be a cult prostitute (*qād̄ēś*) of the sons of Israel."

Deuteronomy 23:18 addresses noncultic prostitution: "You shall not bring the hire of a harlot (*zônâ*) or the wages of a dog (*keleb*), into the house of the LORD your God in payment for any vow; for both of these are an abomination to the LORD your God." "Dog" (*keleb*) in this passage is used as a derogatory term referring to a male prostitute, as is clear from its parallel used with "prostitute" (*zônâ*). Such a derogatorily symbolic meaning for "dog" is not uncommon in the Old Testament, where it is elsewhere used to describe a person's insignificance or to express contempt for one's enemies (for example, 1 Chroni-

cles 17:19; Psalm 22:16, 20). Clearly, male and female prostitution were abominations to Yahweh, Israel's covenant God, and any Israelite practicing this occupation was in violation of the covenant.

Another sexual activity considered deviant in Deuteronomy is transvestism; 22:5 labels such behavior as an abomination to the LORD. This law stipulates that a woman must not put upon herself any utensil *(kelî)* of a man *(geber)*, and a man must not wear the clothing *(simulâ)* of a woman. Since the normal word for "man" in Hebrew is *'îš*, it is instructive that this law employs *geber*, a term typically used to designate the strength of a man as distinct from women, children, and noncombatants. Consistent with this usage is the selection of *kelî* for utensils of a man, for this word frequently refers to "implements of war" or "armor." Thus it appears that the woman was forbidden to assume a manly role or characteristic of strength associated with battle. Similarly, the man was not to assume a feminine role associated with the wearing of a woman's clothing.

Unlike Leviticus 18:22, which refers specifically to homosexuality and labels it as an abomination to God, the transvestism prohibition of Deut. 22:5 probably is another law against worshipping other gods. Evidence from 23:1 indicates that it is possible that transvestism was, like cultic prostitution, associated with certain religious rituals of Israel's neighboring societies, for 23:1 forbids any castrated male from entering into the religious assembly of the LORD. The law could mean that only sexually whole men were acceptable to Yahweh, but it could also be an exclusion of those who had castrated or mutilated themselves as a cultic dedication to some god. H. W. F. Saggs notes that certain temple personnel in Mesopotamia, who wore female clothing during cultic rituals related to the fertility goddess Ishtar, were probably eunuchs.[16] If the exclusion in 23:1 refers to cultic castration, then the ban is based upon religious considerations and not cases of accidental mutilation by otherwise faithful members of Israel's covenant community. This interpretation would eliminate any conflict between 23:1 and the compassionate promise of Isaiah 56:3–5: ". . . let not the eunuch say, 'Behold I am a dry tree.' For thus says the LORD: 'To the eunuchs who . . . hold fast my covenant, I will give in my house . . . a monument and a name better than sons and daughters.' "

The remaining deviant sexual behaviors mentioned in Deuteronomy are incest and bestiality, whose prohibitions are found in 27:20–23.[17] Considered incestuous were intercourse with the wife of one's father, whether she be one's biological mother or otherwise (27:20, 23; cf. 22:30; 23:1).[18] To these actions of incest was added that anyone committing a sexual act with an animal was considered accursed (27:21).

Conclusions

The previous examples of sexual legislation in Deuteronomy reveal that Israel's covenant with God provides the reasons for following the specified sexual regulations. On the one hand these regulations reflect the ideals of a male-dominated agricultural society and thereby have much in common with views held by neighboring societies. On the other hand they reveal strong opposition to the religious practices of surrounding cultures. In the midst of other societies that encourage cultic prostitution, transvestism, and so on, Israel is commanded to practice only heterosexuality within the confines of the marriage relationship. Deviations from this norm are viewed not merely as private acts of personal preference or desire but as breaches of Israel's covenant with Yahweh. To break the covenant is to break an order commanded by God, and this brings God's curse rather than his blessing, not only upon the individual but also upon society as a whole. Consequently, severe measures are to be taken against offenders in order to maintain the blessings of covenant relationship with Yahweh.

The other four books of the Pentateuch (Genesis, Exodus, Leviticus, and Numbers) contain a great deal of information on sexuality that is not found in Deuteronomy. In order to obtain a broader understanding of sexuality in the Pentateuch, it is wise to read through these books. Genesis provides a number of stories that concern sexual practices, and Leviticus details a host of strange, and at times bizarre, rules and rituals dealing with sex. However, in this volume we now turn from the legal material of Deuteronomy to a different type of literature entirely, the Hebrew Wisdom tradition, for another perspective on human sexuality.[19]

1. A storm of controversy surrounds the identity of the author of Deuteronomy as well as the place, date, and purpose of the book. Traditionally Deuteronomy was believed to be almost entirely the work of Moses, but few biblical scholars still maintain this viewpoint. Most Old Testament scholars now fix the time of composition centuries after the time of Moses. For a review of the reasons lying behind the problem of dating the document, consult various Old Testament introductions or commentaries on Deuteronomy.

2. The Hebrews' personal name for God was written with four consonants, YHWH. The Hebrew word is typically transliterated into English as "Yahweh," although many versions of the Bible simply translate it "the LORD."

3. Some translations do not indicate that the wife is the recipient of the joy, and the reader might mistakenly think that this verse is only concerned with the man's pleasure in his wife.

4. This topic is covered in Chapter 3, on Proverbs.

5. The length of time spent in mourning for the dead varied in different time periods of Israelite history. In Deuteronomy it is one month (21:13; 34:8; cf. Numbers 20:29), but in Genesis 50:10 it is seven days (see also 1 Samuel 31:13; 1 Chronicles 10:12).

6. Leviticus 19:26–28 connects rounding off of the hair or beard with witchcraft.

7. Translation by John Gray, *The Legacy of Canaan: The Ras Shamra Texts and Their Relevance to the Old Testament* (Leiden, The Netherlands: E. J. Brill, 1965), p. 252. See also A. Herder, ed., *Corpus des tablettes en cunéiformes alphabetiques*, Mission de Ras Shamra, Tome X. 5.VI.14–18 (=Ugaritic Text 67) on the myth of Baal lacerating himself while mourning over El, and 19.IV.173,184 (=UT 1 Aqht) on professional mourners cutting themselves.

8. This is not the case in other places in the Old Testament. In Nehemiah 10:28–30 and 13:23–27, for example, Nehemiah forces the Jews to divorce the foreign women they have married. However, even in this case the major issue is that of loyalty to Yahweh and his law.

9. On some occasions the land is personified; and, for example, in Leviticus 18:24–30 God punishes the land because it has been defiled by its inhabitants. Numbers 35:33–34 states that the only way land polluted by the shedding of innocent blood (i.e., murder) can be purified is by the shedding of the blood of the murderer.

10. If the man divorced his wife and then decided that he wanted her back, he evidently could remarry her if she had not in the meantime married another.

11. G. J. Wenham, in "Betulah 'A Girl of Marriageable Age,' " *Vetus Testamentum* 22 (1972):326–48, suggests that the husband discovered that his new wife was not menstruating and was suspicious that she was pregnant before he married her. Consequently the parents would be obliged to bring forth bloodstained cloths to prove that she was still menstruating while at home with them. Wenham does not suggest how a judge could tell whether the cloths belonged to the new bride or to other menstruating women in her parents' home.

12. S. R. Driver, *A Critical and Exegetical Commentary on Deuteronomy* (New York: Charles Scribner's Sons, 1895), pp. 255–56.

13. For an extremely similar law in another ancient law code, see Middle Assyrian Law § 55 in James B. Pritchard, ed., *Ancient Near Eastern Texts Relating to the Old Testament* (hereafter *ANET*) (Princeton: Princeton University Press, 1950), p. 185.

14. Cf. *ANET*, p. 171, § 130; p. 162, § 26.

15. Cf. *ANET*, p. 171, § 129; p. 181, laws 12–14; p. 196, § 197; p. 162, § 26.

16. *The Greatness That Was Babylon* (New York: Hawthorn Books, 1962), p. 322. S. R. Driver, *Deuteronomy*, p. 259, cites several examples of religiously inspired mutilation from the later Greco-Roman period: Lucian, *de dea Syria*, § 51; and Bardesanes, *Spicil Syr.*, p. 20, 1:1.

17. Cf. *ANET*, pp. 172f., §§ 154–58.

18. See also Genesis 20:12; 2 Samuel 13:13; Ezekiel 22:11 and the longer list of sexual prohibitions in Leviticus 18:6–18; 20:17–21.

19. Much of Chapter 2 was originally published in *Mind and Nature* 6 (1982): 1–7 under the title "Modern Sexuality and the Biblical Book of Deuteronomy."

Proverbs: a Rational Approach to Sexual Morality

3

Ancient Hebrew
Wisdom Literature

To move from Deuteronomy to Proverbs is to step into an entirely
different literary world, for we move from a law code to a collection of
wise sayings. Deuteronomy is concerned with Israel as a unique people
who have entered into a special covenant with Yahweh, their God. The
laws pertaining to sexual conduct find their basis in this covenant
relationship, and obedience to the covenant stipulations is the foundation for sexual morality. If the Israelites obey the laws, God blesses
them with a good life. If they break the laws, it is a sign of rebellion
against God, and dire consequences will follow. Proverbs, however, is
based not on a covenant motif but on the accumulated wisdom that
results from many years of carefully observing life. The main appeal is
to human reason, not divine command. For example, in Deut. 22:22
we find a law that prescribes the death penalty for men and women
caught in adultery, while in Prov. 5:1–23 we find an attempt to
convince a young man through rational appeal that adultery is a foolish
activity.

Proverbs is similar to Deuteronomy in that it addresses a great number of different aspects of life, but the orientation is distinctly different. There is virtually no stress on Israel's uniqueness or covenant with God. Proverbs focuses not upon covenantal legislation but upon practical advice. Furthermore, whereas Deuteronomy is nationalistic in orientation, Proverbs is universal in scope. The wise men, or sages, who produced Proverbs presupposed a belief in Yahweh; but in this collection of sayings they did not appeal to authoritative laws claiming divine origin. While Deuteronomy's laws are presented as having been given by God to Moses, Proverbs' wise advice is completely written as the product of years of observation of life by people who have carefully studied the way things work in this world. On the one hand Proverbs affirms that "The fear of the LORD (Yahweh) is the beginning of knowledge" (1:7); on the other hand it is perfectly content to look to foreign as well as Hebrew sources of wisdom. We might say that the sages affirmed all truth as God's truth.

The wisdom contained in Proverbs makes no claim to be uniquely that of Israel. Indeed, upon closer inspection we find that Proverbs openly draws upon the wise sayings written by sages in other countries. In looking closely at the composition of the book, we see that approximately seven different collections of material were brought together to produce the present form of Proverbs: (1) 1–9; (2) 10:1–22:16; (3) 22:17–24:34; (4) 25–29; (5) 30:1–33; (6) 31:1–9; (7) 31:10–31. The beginning of each of these sections contains some sort of title, which tells us where one collection ends and the next begins, and each section has its own individual characteristics. Two of the seven sections are clearly designated as non-Israelite in origin: the sayings of Agur, in 30:1–14, and of Lemuel, in 31:1–9. It has also been discovered that a large part of the third collection, Prov. 22:17–24:22, shows literary dependence on an Egyptian text called "The Instruction of Amenemope."[1] For the Hebrew sages, where a saying originated was evidently immaterial. If it was an accurate representation of life, it needed no other validation. Consequently, Proverbs reveals an openness to influence from the wise sayings of other cultures and a readiness to adapt them to Israelite culture.[2]

Such openness should come as no surprise. Since proverbs are short, pithy statements about life that are widely used in virtually all cultures, they are readily adaptable to different languages and societies. Their popularity stems largely from the distilled wisdom they contain. With a minimum number of words, a proverb can elicit graphic mental images:

> Better is a dinner of herbs where love is
> than a fatted ox and hatred with it.
>
> *(15:17)*

> Bread gained by deceit is sweet to a man,
> but afterward his mouth will be full of gravel.
>
> *(20:17)*

> Like a gold ring in a swine's snout
> is a beautiful woman without discretion.
>
> *(11:22)*

> A foolish son is ruin to his father,
> and a wife's quarreling is a continual dripping of rain.
>
> *(19:13)*

> The sluggard buries his hand in the dish,
> and will not even bring it back to his mouth.
>
> *(19:24)*

> The sluggard says, "There is a lion outside!
> I shall be slain in the streets!"
>
> *(22:13)*

The last two sayings make their point against laziness through the use of humorous sarcasm. The pictures of a man who is so lazy he does not even expend enough effort to lift food to his mouth and a person who is always inventing another crazy reason for not going to work are pointed social commentaries. Like the other maxims, they are intended to provoke thought and to inspire acceptable behavior. Merely to hear a

proverb and not to act according to the wisdom it imparts is to negate the purpose for developing such sayings. "Like a lame man's legs, which hang useless, is a proverb in the mouth of fools" (26:7).

When we begin to probe the book of Proverbs for wise teaching in the area of sexual behavior, we observe an interesting fact. There are only occasional statements on this subject in sections two through seven (Prov. 10–31), but section one (Prov. 1–9) contains a large amount of sexually oriented material, so our attention will focus almost entirely on this part of Proverbs. In this first collection of material, which functions as an introduction to the book as a whole, the pages are full of warnings directed to young men to beware of immoral women. Repeatedly employing the literary form of a father instructing his son, Prov. 1–9 seeks to convince young men to order their lives by wisdom and to avoid folly. Appropriately, this section portrays the young man as one who is prone to consider the desires of the moment instead of life as a whole, following impulse instead of reason. And a prime source of temptation toward such folly in this material is the recurring figure of the immoral woman, which the R.S.V. translates "the loose woman." Far from being the innocent party seduced by the male, she is pictured as the seducer of those who do not live wisely.

It is also quite interesting that this first section of Proverbs is not composed of the short, pithy sayings that characterize most of the rest of the book. Primarily comprised of longer discourses that focus heavily on unethical and immoral behaviors that are particularly tempting for young men, this material describes in detail both the pitfalls of such actions and the ways they can be avoided. Proverbs 1–9 reflects a school environment, a setting in which older men sought to teach younger men how to live wisely, and thereby enjoy a long and profitable life.[3] Consequently the material is completely male oriented, for it was designed to address only the male segment of the population.

In spite of this male orientation, Prov. 1–9 also has much to say to women when we understand the theological basis for the teaching it contains. Underlying the instruction directed toward young men is a view of the world that sees all of creation as part of a universal moral order. To live in harmony with this all-pervasive order is to live wisely

and thereby to experience the best in life.[4] But to go against God's order is to live foolishly and to court disaster; for when the order is defied, negative consequences will surely follow. This applies to women as well as to men; so although the specific teaching of Prov. 1–9 is directed to men, the principles for wise living contained in this material apply equally to women. If a woman lives wantonly, she will experience disastrous consequences just like a man, so she must also be wise in her approach to life.

The Hebrew sages believed that God himself employed wisdom when he created the world and that he established orderly patterns in creation. This belief is given clear expression in several passages in Prov. 1–9:

> The LORD by wisdom founded the earth;
>   by understanding he established the heavens;
> by his knowledge the deeps broke forth,
>   and the clouds drop the dew.
>
> *(3:19–20)*

What 3:19–20 asserts forthrightly, 8:22–31 expresses poetically by personifying Wisdom and allowing her to sing her own praises, exalting her role in creation. Through poetic repetition this passage stresses that before God ever began his first act of creation, Wisdom was his prized possession. When he created the mountains and seas and heavens and all the universe, he did so by the use of Wisdom. From the perspective of Prov. 1–9 the implication is very clear: If God employed wisdom to create the world, then the only way to live in harmony with God's order is to govern all of life by wisdom.

For those people who love Wisdom and follow her ways, she promises a long and happy life in the favor of the LORD (8:32–36). Such an existence is not the unique possession of a group of scholars either, as 8:1–21 clearly reveals. In this passage Wisdom cries aloud at the most public places in the city to all who will listen, inviting them to come and learn her ways of truth and morality. Those who reject her summons have only themselves to blame when calamity comes on them suddenly like a terrible storm (1:20–33). In their distress, fools may

cry out for Wisdom with tears, but it will then be too late. Foolish behavior brings destruction—they must suffer the consequences of their actions. Whereas in Deuteronomy breaking the law brings about the curses of God due to breach of the covenant, in Proverbs living immorally puts a person at odds with divine order, and negative consequences are a built-in part of the system. Thus, in Deuteronomy, sexual deviance equals covenant infidelity, but in Proverbs it is primarily equated with ignorance.

Wisdom or Folly: Choosing Which Woman to Love

To avoid the wiles of the loose woman, young men are encouraged in Prov. 1–9 to consider the long-term consequences of sexual immorality, not to focus on the enticing desire of the moment in isolation. Youth, with their strong sexual desires, are rather impetuous and tend to ignore the dangerous implications of their actions. As a result they often experience a great amount of misery that could have been avoided. Due to the function of Prov. 1–9 as an attempt to persuade youth to order their lives wisely, it is interesting that this collection of material deals with only one basic form of sexual deviance: that of a foolish young man falling prey to the seduction of an adulterous woman.

There are a number of warnings in Prov. 1–9 against the activities of such women, including several stylized stories of seduction developed for instructional purposes. But the educational function of this first section of Proverbs may be seen in yet another use of female imagery. At times the material contains personifications of the two directions in life a person may choose to go: the way of wisdom and the way of folly. These two directions are symbolized as two women who seek the lives of young men. Both are very appealing, but in different ways. The first is an elegant woman who openly seeks people in public places in broad daylight. She is Wisdom, personified as a stately lady, who offers the best things in life to all who will choose to follow her.

The second is a brash woman who roams around, often at night, seeking to seduce foolish young men into the delights of wickedness. She offers extremely enticing covert pleasures, but those who yield to her wiles discover only death.

These two women represent two paths along which a person may walk through life: the road of wisdom, which is paved with righteousness and justice and leads to life (2:8–11, 20–22; 4:11–13, 18); and the highway of folly, which is paved with perversion and leads to death (2:12–19; 4:14–17, 19). To follow the path of wisdom is to recognize that God has established a moral order in the world. People living in harmony with God's order will experience his blessing, but those who live foolishly go against God's created order and bring their lives to ruin. Consequently, quality of life is the result of which path a person decides to follow, or, expressed symbolically, which woman a man chooses to love.

The contrast between these two women is vividly revealed in Prov. 9, where Wisdom personified is juxtaposed with Folly personified. In 9:1–6 Wisdom is portrayed as an elegant lady who has prepared a marvelous feast with the best of meat and wine on her magnificent tables. Doing everything properly, she sends her maids out to deliver the invitation to her feast, and they go to the most public places of the city. In spite of the grand nature of the banquet, it is not exclusive, but is open for all to attend. The foolish are invited to come and enjoy all that Wisdom has to offer. They need only recognize their folly and leave it behind in order to taste the good life offered by Wisdom.

Folly, on the other hand, is pictured in 9:13–18 as the absolute contrast to Wisdom. She is a shameless woman who is loud and boisterous. Verse 13a uses a participial form of the Hebrew verb *hāmâ*, a term frequently used for the growling and barking of animals, in order to describe her brazen behavior. From the doorstep of her ill-reputed house and from the busiest parts of the city she addresses passersby with the same invitation employed by Wisdom's messengers: "Whoever is simple, let him turn in here!" (9:4, 16). But the feast Folly offers is pitiful by comparison. Whereas Wisdom provides a righteous banquet

of choice meat, bread, and wine, Folly advertises only water and bread. She makes her paltry fare attractive, however, by appealing to the covert nature of her meal: "Stolen water is sweet, and bread eaten in secret is pleasant" (9:17). Seductively, Folly promises that forbidden pleasures are sweeter than those enjoyed legally at the house of Wisdom, and fools ignorantly fall for her fraudulent speech. They settle for something far less desirable only because of a deceptively enticing appeal. This description of Folly ominously ends with the warning that the fools who secretively go to Folly's house do not realize that death lurks behind her doors.

The author of Prov. 1–9 fully understood the tempting nature of covert sexual activity for young men, and he employed the imagery of Folly as a seductive woman in order to communicate his point powerfully. Although Folly may seem attractive, ultimately she has nothing to offer except misery and death. If a young man would follow Wisdom, he could see through the deception of Folly. As we will see later, the wise man is the one who fully enjoys sexual intercourse with his own wife. Only the fool seeks illicit sexual encounters with other women.

Sexual Immorality: Recognizing the Trap of the Loose Woman

Closely identified with Lady Folly in Prov. 9:13–18 are the recurring descriptions of the adulterous woman in Prov. 1–7. Such a woman lives on the foolish road to death, and she draws all who come to her into the same fate (2:16–19). Described as a foreign or strange woman (*îshâ zārâ*, 2:16a) and an alien (*nākrîyâ*, 2:16b), her dominant characteristic is her "smooth words." She is a smooth talker, having developed the art of convincing men to share covert sexual activities with her. Deceptive and deadly, she lures foolish men into her trap.

We should not assume that the stereotyped "strange" or "alien" woman in Proverbs is a non-Israelite.[5] She is strange or foreign because she belongs to someone else, and sexual intercourse with her is not

legitimate.[6] The R.S.V. calls her the loose woman, and this is an accurately descriptive designation of her moral condition. A strange woman in Prov. 1–7 is any woman whom a man might encounter who would lure him into illegal sexual relations, but the primary reference is to married women who are unfaithful to their husbands.

Adultery is in view in 2:16–19, where the "strange woman" is said to have forsaken the companion of her youth and forgotten the covenant of her God. Since Hebrew girls were usually married shortly after puberty, often about one year after they began to menstruate, the expression "companion of her youth" most likely designates her husband (cf. 5:18 "wife of your youth"). An adulteress, she has broken the covenant with God by transgressing the seventh commandment: "You shall not commit adultery" (Deut. 5:18).[7] Malachi 2:14–16 uses similar language to condemn divorce:

> The LORD was witness to the covenant between you and the wife of your youth, to whom you have been faithless, though she is your companion and your wife by covenant. Has not the one God made and sustained for us the spirit of life? And what does he desire? Godly offspring. So take heed to yourselves, and let none be faithless to the wife of his youth. "For I hate divorce, says the LORD the God of Israel. . . . So take heed to yourselves and do not be faithless."

Although *covenant* in this passage from Malachi refers to the actual marriage contract, not to Israel's covenant with God, and although the accusation is against the men of Malachi's day who were divorcing their wives (an option not available to the women), not against a woman who has forsaken her husband, the theme of faithlessness to the mate of one's youth is so similar to Prov. 2:17 that it aids in illuminating the activity of the "strange woman." She is an adulteress who has turned her back on her husband and her God, a seductively smooth talker (2:16) who not only treads the road to destruction herself but also leads others along the same path (2:18–19). To possess her is to embrace death.[8]

In 5:1–6 the wise educator states that a young man can be saved from the strange woman if he orders his life by wisdom. This passage

warns that, although the strange woman may be very persuasive, it is absolute folly to listen to her. Only wisdom can equip a man to understand that her seductive speech, which is so sweet and enticing, hides the bitter results of believing what she says. Her lips "drip honey," and her words are "smoother than oil" (5:3), "but in the end she is bitter as wormwood, sharp as a two-edged sword" (5:4). She ignores God's created order in her wanton behavior, ignorant of the fact that she is on the path to *Sheol* (5:5–6).

For the ancient Hebrews, Sheol designated the silent realm of the dead, located in some huge subterranean vault.[9] They believed that *all* people went there permanently when they died (Psalm 89:48), where they had some undefined, shadowy existence, removed from and unaware of God's actions and therefore unable to praise God.[10] As a people the Hebrews speculated very little on the nature of existence in Sheol, for they viewed the land of the living as the realm in which God was active. Consequently, they thought that if God was going to bless someone, it would be during that person's lifetime, a belief that comes to clear expression in a prayer to God in Psalm 6:4–5: "Turn, O LORD, save my life. . . . For in death there is no remembrance of thee, in Sheol who can give thee praise?" At death all people, the good and the bad, went to this underground vault, which was described in terms similar to those used in Babylonian mythology. The Babylonians believed that the throat of the god Mot formed the entrance to the subterranean realm of the dead,[11] a concept reflected in Prov. 1:12, where robbers compare their murderous activity to the gaping throat of Sheol when they say of their victims, "Like Sheol let us swallow them alive."

With no expectation of a blessed afterlife in the presence of God,[12] the sages who produced Prov. 1–9 viewed a long and prosperous life as evidence of God's blessing upon a person.[13] Therefore in 5:8–14 the wise elder counsels young men to stay far away from strange women lest their lives be cut short by dissolute living:

> . . . do not go near the door of her house; lest you give . . . your years to the merciless . . . and at the end of your life you groan, when your

flesh and body are consumed, and you say, "How I hated discipline. . . . I did not listen to the voice of my teachers. . . .",

The elder warns that loose living will place you into the company of those who care nothing for your well-being (5:9–10). Mercilessly your so-called friends will take whatever they can get out of you, and your life will end in shambles. What begins as "fun" ends up being deadly. It is even possible that the reference in 5:11 to the consumption of a person's flesh is an allusion to venereal disease.

Sexual Contentment: Knowing How to Avoid Immorality

All of this misery, which results from an illegitimate pursuit of sexual pleasure, can be avoided if a man will simply live in faithfulness to his own wife. The educator, in poetically symbolic language, tells the young man to limit his sexual activity to his wife alone: "Drink water from your own cistern, flowing water from your own well" (5:15). This imagery is similar to Song of Songs 4:15, where the woman is called "a garden fountain, a well of living water." In the arid climate of Palestine, a drink of cool water was sometimes used to symbolize that which was not only enjoyable but also life-sustaining. Thus, when the sage counsels the young man to drink water from his own well, he means that the youth should drink deeply of the physical pleasures of his own wife.

The imagery in 5:16–17 continues in water metaphors, but now they apply to the man, and interpreting their meaning is difficult:

> Should your springs be scattered abroad,
> 　　streams of water in the streets?
> Let them be for yourself alone,
> 　　and not for strangers with you.

In the Hebrew it is not clear whether 5:16 is a question or a command, since there is no change in sentence construction between verses 15 and

16. The R.S.V. translates it as a sarcastic question, and the meaning would consequently be something like, "Should you scatter your semen in the streets among strangers?" W. McKane points to the parallel imagery of Sirach 26:19–21 to justify this interpretation.[14]

> My son, keep sound the bloom of your youth, and do not give your strength to strangers. Seek a fertile field within the whole plain, and sow it with your seed, trusting in your fine stock. So your offspring will survive and, having confidence in their good descent, will grow great.

If, on the other hand, 5:16 is a command, it would probably mean that a man should beget many children, who would flow out like streams of water from a fertile wife whose husband stays home and does not squander his potency elsewhere.[15] This would fit the general belief that having many children was a great blessing, as we saw in Deuteronomy, and as is vividly expressed in Psalm 127:3–5:

> Lo, sons are a heritage from the LORD, the fruit of the womb a reward. Like arrows in the hand of a warrior are the sons of one's youth. Happy is the man who has his quiver full of them!

Nevertheless, regardless of whether Prov. 5:16 is a question or a command, the overall point of the passage is very clear: *Stay home!*

Note again how different is the educational approach of Prov. 1–9 from the legislation of Deuteronomy. Both documents promote basically the same views on sexuality; but whereas Deuteronomy states that an act is wrong and designates a punishment for it, Proverbs employs reason to convince people that moral behavior is the best way to live. For example, in Prov. 5 the educator attempts to diminish the temptation of a young man being led astray by a loose woman by temporarily directing the focus away from the temptress toward the youth's own wife.

> . . . rejoice in the wife of your youth,
>   a lovely hind, a graceful doe.
> Let her affection fill you at all times with delight,
>   be infatuated always with her love.

(5:18–19)

There are three directives in this passage that will lead to legitimate sexual contentment, thereby reducing desire for illegitimate sexual adventure: (1) seek to appreciate fully the beauty of your own wife; (2) take great delight in your wife's body (the Hebrew of 5:19 literally reads, "Let her *breasts* satisfy [or delight] you at all times"); and (3) be so in love with your wife that you are "intoxicated" with her. The verb translated "infatuated" in 5:19c by the R.S.V., *šāgâ*, means to reel as a drunken person.[16] Thus the sage counsels men to take such physical delight in loving their wives that the resulting satisfaction will keep them from the folly of following loose women.

> Why should you be infatuated (*šāgâ*), my son with a loose woman
>   and embrace the bosom of an adventuress?
> For a man's ways are before the eyes of the LORD,
>   and he watches all his paths.
> The iniquities of the wicked ensnare him,
>   and he is caught in the toils of his sin.
> He dies for lack of discipline,
>   and because of his great folly he is lost.
>
> *(5:20–23)*

"Why," asks the wise man, "should you reel with intoxicated desire for a strange woman and embrace her breasts when you have your own wife?" Such activities may begin with a brief fling in the night, but over a period of time they become a trap in which a man is snared (5:22). Little threads soon become restricting ropes! Furthermore, what is accomplished in secret, hidden from the knowledge of other people, is plainly visible to the eyes of God. Here we catch a glimpse of divine retribution in Proverbs: The LORD observes those who commit sexual immorality, and they die because of their sin.

Adultery: Reckoning with the Danger

So strongly does the author of Prov. 1–9 view the adulteress as a major temptation for young men, and so dreadful does he believe the consequences of adultery to be, that he devotes 6:20–7:27 to yet another

extended warning against following the loose woman. Again the educator mentions the smooth speech of the adulteress (6:24), but this time he focuses on more than her seductive speech:

> Do not desire her beauty in your heart,
> and do not let her capture you with her eyelashes;
> for a harlot may be hired for a loaf of bread,
> but an adulteress stalks a man's very life.
> Can a man carry fire in his bosom
> and his clothes not be burned?
> Or can one walk upon hot coals
> and his feet not be scorched?
> So is he who goes in to his neighbor's wife;
> none who touches her will go unpunished.
> . . . For jealousy makes a man furious,
> and he will not spare when he takes revenge.
>
> *(6:25–29, 34)*

A beautiful woman who knows how to flirt with her eyes can lure a man into foolish actions. When she offers herself to him through seductive verbal and nonverbal communication, he is tempted to take chances he otherwise might not consider. For almost any heterosexual man there is something thrilling about an attractive woman communicating to him that she desires him. Not only is the chase exhilarating, but seeing that she desires him is gratifying to his ego. The consequences of yielding to such impulses are, however, absolutely devastating.

Our wise old sage asserts that locating a prostitute is much safer by comparison. You can pay her fee and go your way. Adultery, on the other hand, although it does not involve the payment of money, is far more costly. To embrace another man's wife is to embrace fire, and there is no way to avoid getting burned by the encounter. Sex with a prostitute can be a very impersonal matter: She can be nothing more than a body to be used. But this sort of depersonalization is not possible with your neighbor's wife. There is an extended web of relationships involving your own wife, children, parents, and extended family, as well as her husband and all her extended family—not to mention other

neighbors, business associates, friends, the religious community, and so forth. What two people try to accomplish in secret may easily be discovered, and suddenly a great number of people are hurt.

When we recall that for the ancient Hebrews a man's wife was his property and that he placed great emphasis on her bearing legitimate offspring for him, the description of the rage of the offended husband in 6:33–35 is no surprise. As a result of the thrill of a brief, covert sexual encounter with another man's wife, the guilty young man experiences public disgrace, financial disaster, and perhaps death itself. In order to illustrate this point, the educator points out the consequences of a compulsive act far less serious than adultery:

> Do not men despise a thief if he steals
>   to satisfy his appetite when he is hungry?
> And if he is caught, he will pay sevenfold;
>   he will give all the goods of his house.
> He who commits adultery has no sense;
>   he who does it destroys himself.
> Wounds and dishonor will he get,
>   and his disgrace will not be wiped away.
> For jealousy makes a man furious,
>   and he will not spare when he takes revenge.
> He will accept no compensation,
>   nor be appeased though you multiply gifts.
>
> *(6:30–35)*

If a thief is hungry and steals food, he is not pitied because he stole to satisfy his appetite.[17] If caught, he will have to pay for his crime far beyond the actual value of the food he stole.[18] The adulterer, however, is unable to compensate for his crime, even if he offers large sums of money to the offended husband. Inflamed with jealousy, the husband will show no mercy when he takes revenge.

All this misery may be avoided if a young man will but listen to the wise teaching of his elders and order his life by wisdom (6:20–24). Like a light, wisdom illuminates the long-range implications of illegal sexual intercourse and helps a person to see beyond the immediate desire (6:23). How much human misery is caused by the self-deception

of thinking that immediate gratifying of desire will have no future consequences? How many times do people choose to disregard reason and possess what is forbidden, whether it be sex or something else very enticing? How often does the forbidden fruit that seems so sweet turn out to be rotten, causing lifelong heartbreak, not just for those directly involved but for others as well? "Beware my child. Do not be deceived. Love wisdom and she will give you a long and happy life. Love folly and you will dwell in misery."

The Seduction: Recounting a Sad Tale

To illustrate how attractive adultery can be, and how much a person needs wisdom, the wise educator recounts a graphic story of seduction in 7:6–27. Once again prefacing the story by stressing that wisdom can preserve a man from the smooth words of the strange woman (7:1–5), he tells how such a woman entices a foolish young man. In the tale a youth is wandering rather aimlessly in the area of her house in the darkness of night, and he lacks the sense to know the danger. Although the youth's course is aimless, the adulterous woman's is not. With a well-defined purpose she skillfully stalks her prey. Dressed seductively, her manner brazen, like a prostitute, she is "the huntress," and Derek Kidner summarizes her ability well when he comments, "It will be an unequal contest."[19]

Lying in wait at the street corner, the adulteress springs into action as the youth walks by:

> She seizes him and kisses him,
>   and with impudent face she says to him:
> "I had to offer sacrifices,
>   and today I have paid my vows:
> So now I have come out to meet you,
>   to seek you eagerly, and I have found you.
> I have decked my couch with coverings,
>   colored spreads of Egyptian linen;

I have perfumed my bed with myrrh,
　aloes, and cinnamon.
Come, let us take our fill of love till morning;
　let us delight ourselves with love.
For my husband is not at home;
　he has gone on a long journey. . . ."

(7:13–20)

So convincing is her story that the young man would think himself a fool if he did not respond positively. At her home is a large quantity of freshly cooked meat, for on that very day she had slaughtered an animal in fulfillment of some sacrificial religious ceremony. In addition, there is the lure of the elegantly made and sensuously scented bed of the temptress, which she describes as a perfumed paradise wherein the youth can enjoy a night of total bliss. And it is all free—and safe. Her husband is out of town, with no chance of his returning to find them together. How absolutely tempting! A great meal, an exciting night with a strange woman, and no one else will ever know.

How will the young man respond? He knows that the woman is cheating on her husband, and obviously she is a brazen type who has few religious consistencies. The nature of the vows she took in conjunction with her sacrificial offering is uncertain; but if we are to understand from this stylized story that she is a Hebrew, then she represents a type of person whose religious confession is antithetical to her actual life-style. Like a great many people today, she continues to practice the religious ceremonies she learned as a child, although she has abandoned the ethical and moral codes of her Hebrew faith. By offering sacrifice, she is performing a religious activity that is expected of members of God's covenant people, people who are to maintain high sexual standards. Yet during the very act of sacrificing, she is already planning how to use the meat as part of her covert sexual activities on that same night. For her the following proverbs apply:

The sacrifice of the wicked is an abomination to the
　LORD. . . .

(15:8)

The sacrifice of the wicked is an abomination;
how much more *when he brings it with evil intent*.

(21:27) *(italics mine)*

This loose woman is certainly not the sort that the young man would want as a wife, but what about a free evening of food and sex with her? Momentarily he hesitates, considering the situation, but her reassuring words prove to be too overpowering. *Folly prevails!*

With much seductive speech she persuades him;
with her smooth talk she compels him.
All at once he follows her,
as an ox goes to the slaughter,
or as a stag is caught fast
till an arrow pierces its entrails;
as a bird rushes into a snare;
he does not know that it will cost him his life.

(7:21–23)

The cumulative effect of her words diminishes whatever resistance the young man had, compelling him to follow her. He probably envisions himself as wise to take advantage of such a safe and delightful affair, but the storyteller compares the youth to a dumb animal being led to its death. Unwittingly he follows the countless number of men who have preceded him in such acts of folly, only to join them in ruining his life and coming to an untimely death.

Let not your heart turn aside to her ways,
do not stray into her paths;
for many a victim has she laid low;
yea, all her slain are a mighty host.
Her house is the way to Sheol,
going down to the chambers of death.

(7:25–27)

Had the youth followed Wisdom, she would have preserved him from such a fate, allowing him to see through the beautiful outward appearance of Folly to the hideous ugliness lurking behind her gilded doors.

The seduction story almost forces the question: "What would I do if I encountered a similar situation, and upon what basis would I make my decision?" Our wise old sage would point us first to the social consequences involved, but there is yet another dimension. Standing behind the moral order of creation is the creator, God, watching. When making moral decisions, a person must reckon with the presence of this One who instituted the universal order, a system based on Wisdom.

Proverbs 10–31: Observing Some Final Practical Advice

There are only a few sayings that address sexual issues in the six distinct sections of Proverbs contained in chapters 10–31. As we might expect, there are several proverbs that reveal the Hebrews' wholehearted approval of marriage:

> He who finds a wife finds a good thing,
>   and obtains favor from the LORD.
>
> (18:22)

> House and wealth are inherited from fathers,
>   but a prudent wife is from the LORD.
>
> (19:14)

Accompanying these blessings upon marriage and sexual relations within its bonds, there are condemnations of prostitution and adultery:

> The mouth of a loose woman is a deep pit;
>   he with whom the LORD is angry will fall into it.
>
> (22:14)[20]

> . . . a harlot (*zônâ*) is a deep pit;
>   an adventuress is a narrow well.
> She lies in wait like a robber
>   and increases the faithless among men.
>
> (23:27–28)

The latter proverb repeats the picture we saw earlier of the woman actively seeking her prey, only now she is portrayed as a robber waiting for a victim. Comparing the adulteress and prostitute to a deep and narrow hole into which a man falls and is unable to climb out, Prov. 22:14 and 23:27–28 repeat in a different way the same warning of doom involved in encounters with such women in Prov. 1–7.[21]

The economic liability of visiting prostitutes is mentioned in 29:3: "He who loves wisdom makes his father glad, but the one who keeps company with harlots squanders his substance." Perhaps the most pointed remark is found in 30:20: "This is the way of the adulteress: she eats, and wipes her mouth, and says, 'I have done nothing wrong.' " In this comment she represents someone so degraded that she is as at ease with her adultery as she is with eating a meal.[22] For her, both are merely physical satisfaction.[23] After she eats, she wipes her mouth, and that is the end of the matter; so it is with her adultery.[24] It is even possible that eating in 30:20 is a euphemism for sexual intercourse.[25]

Section six of Proverbs (31:1–9) is written in the literary form of a mother giving wise advice to her son the king, with part of her advice concerning the time he spends with his royal harem: "Give not your strength to women, your ways to those who destroy kings" (31:3). In effect the mother is cautioning her son against exhausting his strength by spending so much time with his harem that he is rendered unfit to discharge his governing responsibilities as king. The saying almost certainly does not reflect a negative view of sex or even of polygamy. It is merely a caution against overindulgence with women, much as the next two verses (31:4–5) caution against overindulgence with wine.

Conclusions

Although Proverbs does not deal with the variety of sexual practices that Deuteronomy does, it contains largely the same set of sexual ethics. Sexual relations within marriage are good and are to be enjoyed, but sexual encounters outside of marriage are an affront to God and wisdom (that is, common sense). Whereas Deuteronomy *legislates*

against sexual deviance and prescribes punishments for offenses, Proverbs *educates* against sexual deviance and warns of the deadly consequences incurred from such actions. Sexual relations outside of marriage violate God's created order, and those who practice such license go against the order that preceded the creation of the world. The universe is moral to its very core; and to experience the best from life, people must live in moral harmony with this all-pervasive order. Thus, Proverbs offers advice, not legislation, and this advice is based on careful observation of life as lived.

The educator(s) who compiled Prov. 1–9 sought to instill within young men the desire to order their lives by Wisdom, not Folly. Wisdom allows a person to see life as a whole and make intelligent decisions based on an understanding of God's moral order. Folly, on the other hand, causes a person to focus on the desires of the moment, being duped into making decisions based on what is tempting. By focusing on what a person wants *now*, Folly blinds the individual to the long-range consequences of immoral actions, hiding the hideous specter of death that lurks behind the attractive outward facade. Wisdom, by contrast, enables a person to see that a long and happy life results from living in harmony with the moral order of the world.

Notes

1. For a complete discussion of the literary dependence of Prov. 22:17–24:22 on Amenemope, see Glendon E. Bryce, *A Legacy of Wisdom: The Egyptian Contribution to the Wisdom of Israel* (Lewisburg, Penn.: Bucknell University Press, 1979), especially pp. 15–56.

2. Ibid., pp. 57–134.

3. E.g., 3:1–2, 9–10.

4. E.g., 3:19; 8:1–36.

5. In Deuteronomy 25:5 and Job 19:15, the term *stranger* designates a person who is not part of one's own clan or immediate family.

6. See Prov. 2:16; 5:3, 10, 17, 20; 6:1; 7:5; 11:15; 14:10; 20:16; 22:14; 23:33; 27:2, 13, for the variety of ways in which *strange* is used.

7. William McKane, *Proverbs: A New Approach* (Philadelphia: Westminster Press, 1970), p. 286, argues that the companion of the woman's youth is her father, who taught her how to behave but whose advice she now spurns.

8. For this woman the term "alien" (*nākrîyâ*, 2:16) is figurative for the illegal nature of relationship with her. "Strange" occurs nine times in Proverbs (2:16; 5:10, 20; 6:24; 7:5; 20:16; 23:27; 27:2, 13), and in seven of these instances it is used in parallel with "strange woman" and is apparently employed as a synonym. Its meaning is parallel to "strange woman," consistently expressing the meaning of strangeness or unfamiliarity, not "alien" as in non-Israelite. Cf. Isaiah 28:21 where *nākrîyâ* describes God's wrath upon Israel as his "strange deed" (*zār ma'aśēbû*) and "unfamiliar" work (*nākrîyâ*), i.e., God's wrath is an unfamiliar action.

9. E.g., Numbers 16:30; Jonah 2:6.

10. Psalms 88:3–6, 10–12; 94:17; 115:17; 30:9; Job 3:17; 7:9–10; 10:20–21; 16:22; Ecclesiastes 12:5; Isaiah 14:9.

11. See McKane, *Proverbs*, pp. 269–70, 287–88.

12. By the first century A.D. many Jews believed that upon dying, a good person went to Paradise to await the resurrection of the dead, but the wicked went to the subterranean Hades to await judgment and destruction. See Luke 16:23, 26; 23:43; Josephus, *War* III. 375; and "An Extract Out of Josephus' Discourse to the Greeks Concerning Hades." The Sadducees, however, rejected these beliefs in afterlife as liberal new ideas with no basis in the law of Moses.

13. Later Hebrew Wisdom writers challenged this belief, for they were painfully aware that a good person may suffer even if he or she has not sinned. The book of Job explores this problem of innocent suffering, and the author of Ecclesiastes questions God's involvement in such matters. By 40 B.C. the author(s) of the Psalms of Solomon combines present and future retribution, claiming that God preserves the righteous in this life and raises them from the dead, but he pours out his wrath on the wicked while they live and then denies them resurrection (Psalms of Solomon 3:9–12; 13:5–12; 14:1–10 in the Septuagint).

14. McKane, *Proverbs*, p. 319.

15. Cf. A. Cohen, *Proverbs* (London: The Soncino Press, 1952), p. 28. Derek Kidner, *The Proverbs* (London: Inter-Varsity Press, 1964), p. 70, takes it to mean the flowing blessings of a true family.

16. E.g., Prov. 20:1; Isaiah 28:7.

17. It is also possible to translate Prov. 6:30, "Men do not despise a thief if he

steals when he is hungry." If this translation is adopted, the indication would be that even though the man is not despised for his action, he still must pay dearly. The adulterer, however, is despised for his behavior (6:33).

18. Justice in the Old Testament involved the guilty party making restitution to the injured party. See, e.g., Exodus 22:1–8 (21:37–22:8 in the Hebrew text).

19. Kidner, *Proverbs*, p. 75.

20. Prov. 10:1–22:16 as a whole reveals a rather deterministic theological viewpoint, and 22:14 reflects this outlook (cf. 16:1, 4, 9, 33; 19:21; 21:1, 30–31).

21. Prov. 5:9–14, 22–23; 6:26–35; 7:22–27.

22. Kidner, *Proverbs*, p. 180.

23. Cohen, *Proverbs*, p. 205.

24. McKane, *Proverbs*, p. 658.

25. R. B. Y. Scott, *Proverbs and Ecclesiastes*, The Anchor Bible (Garden City, N.Y.: Doubleday & Co., Inc., 1965), p. 181.

Song of Songs: a Celebration of the Sensuous

4

Ancient Hebrew Love Poetry

Turning to the Song of Songs (also called the Song of Solomon) after studying Deuteronomy and Proverbs is like picking up a romance novel after reading a law book and a volume of popularized philosophy. Suddenly we are removed from the world of concern for right and wrong and the realm of rational contemplation of the consequences of our behavior. We find ourselves in a sea of emotional expression, rolling up and down as wave after wave of descriptions of passion and desire surge past. The Song of Songs (hereinafter also called the Song) is a collection of poems of unknown origin, in which most of the content consists of the words of men and women speaking of love, desire, and praise either to or about their lovers. Except for a few instances, such as when a man calls his lady "my bride" (for example, 4:9, 10, 11, 12; 5:1), the poems do not even specify that the loving couples are married, although in light of Jewish cultural norms we might reasonably expect that this is presupposed. There is no concern here to explore questions of ethics. Indeed, God's name is never mentioned in the Song, and there is no theological reflection at all.[1] Considerations of the best way

to navigate on the sea of life are ignored completely. Here there is only the pure enjoyment of playing in the water.

The Song is a celebration of the sensuous. Focusing on the joys and longing of love and physical passion, it is so sexual that, when the Jewish rabbis were deciding which documents were to be included in the canon of Scripture, there was some debate over whether or not to admit this collection of love poetry. These men were not the only ones to feel a little nervous about inclusion of the Song in the Bible. Even today the uninhibited erotic symbolism in this document continues to raise eyebrows, and many a religious teacher is rather unsure as to how to use it, if at all.

For those who tend to devalue the human body and desire to place their existence almost entirely on a spiritual plane, the Song can be, very frankly, an embarrassment. The overtly sexual nature of the poems, in which the characters speak of strong physical passion, desire, and fulfillment, proclaims unashamedly the joys of the erotic aspects of life. For example, in the Song we have a series of intimate statements made by lovers to each other. In one of these exchanges the man says,

> How fair and pleasant you are,
> O loved one, delectable maiden!
> You are stately as a palm tree,
> and your breasts are like its clusters.
> I say I will climb the palm tree
> and lay hold of its branches.
> Oh, may your breasts be like clusters of the vine,
> and the scent of your breath like apples,
> and your kisses like the best wine
> that goes down smoothly,
> gliding over lips and teeth.
>
> *(7:6–9)*

And the woman responds warmly to his sexual advances:

> I am my beloved's,
> and his desire is for me.

Come, my beloved,
　　let us go forth into the fields,
　　and lodge in the villages. . . .
There I will give you my love.
The mandrakes give forth fragrance,
　　and over our doors are all choice fruits,
new as well as old,
　　which I have laid up for you, O my beloved.

(7:10–13)

The Song can also present problems to people who believe that reasons for wanting to marry someone should exclude almost entirely any concern over whether or not a person finds his or her potential mate physically attractive. According to such a viewpoint, marriage should be based almost exclusively on the spiritual qualities of the husband or wife. You may well imagine the frustration of people who espouse such a view when they read the lengthy descriptions of physical beauty given in the Song. Using vivid poetic imagery, the characters in the poems proclaim the beauty of their loved ones, a phenomenon we shall explore in detail later but that may be illustrated now with a few brief quotations:

Behold, you are beautiful, my love;
　　behold, you are beautiful;
　　your eyes are doves.
Behold, you are beautiful, my beloved,
　　truly lovely. . . .

(1:15–16)

As a lily among brambles,
　　so is my love among maidens.

(2:2)

As an apple tree among the trees of the wood,
　　so is my beloved among young men.
With great delight I sat in his shadow,
　　and his fruit was sweet to my taste.

(2:3)

There are sixty queens and eighty concubines,
    and maidens without number.
My dove, my perfect one, is only one,
    the darling of her mother,
    flawless to her that bore her.

(6:8–9)

Not only do the lovers describe each other's beauty, but they also express longing. For example, after admitting that she is sick with love (2:5), the woman enunciates her desire that her lover hold and fondle her:

O that his left hand were under my head,
    and that his right hand embraced me!

(2:6 cf. 8:3)

Actually, the Song both begins and ends with a woman voicing her longing to be possessed by her lover:

O that you would kiss me with the kisses of your mouth!
For your love is better than wine,
    your anointing oils are fragrant,
your name is oil poured out;
    therefore the maidens love you.
Draw me after you, let us make haste.

(1:2–4)

Make haste, my beloved,
    and be like a gazelle
or a young stag
    upon the mountains of spices.

(8:14)

The woman's adoration of her lover knows no bounds, and her invitation to him in 8:14 is couched in sexual imagery, as a similar imagery in the exchange between lovers in 2:8–17 makes very clear. In this passage she compares her lover to a young stag bounding up and down over the mountains, headed toward her house. Upon his arrival he

speaks romantically to her, inviting her to come away with him. Employing the imagery of springtime in his language of love, he tells her that the rainy weather of winter is over and that the land has burst forth with all the glories of spring. The young man informs his loving lady that flowers have covered the ground, and the air is full of the sounds of turtledoves, who return each year in the spring. Everywhere is the sweet smell of blossoming grapevines, and figs have appeared on the fig trees. It is a wonderful and romantic time of the year!

Following his explanation of the sweet conditions of spring, in 2:14 the young man compares his lady to a dove timidly hiding in a cliff, and he coaxes her to come out of her place of refuge. Since doves are known to build their nests in cleft places in cliffs and, when frightened, to hide in such locations,[2] the poetic imagery is very vivid. Tenderly he seeks to draw the young lady out of her hiding place into the warm spring sunshine where he can see her beautiful face and hear her lovely voice. Then he adds what is for us a rather enigmatic statement:

> Catch us the foxes,
>   the little foxes,
> that spoil the vineyards,
>   for our vineyards are in blossom.
>
> (2:15)

Apparently it was a common plague to have foxes creep in at night and pillage the vineyards. Referring to such destruction, the lover invites his lady to help him remove from their vineyards (that is, themselves) those things that would spoil their ability to enjoy the springtime delights of their love. In other words, he tells her that they are in full blossom, ready to experience the fruit of love. Therefore she should come out of hiding and chase away any little inhibiting "foxes" that might keep them apart.

The woman's response is all that her lover has requested. She emerges from her place of refuge and says,

My beloved is mine and I am his,
   he pastures his flock among the lilies.
Until the day breathes
   and the shadows flee,
turn, my beloved, be like a gazelle,
   or a young stag upon the rugged mountains.

(2:16–17)

In this reply she compares her body to a delightful place where he can pasture his sheep, then she likens herself to the mountains on which a young stag dwells. Whether this second metaphor indicates another image of food, deriving meaning from the fact that a stag browses upon the mountains as a sheep grazes among lilies, or whether it is an allusion to playful frolicking, such as that of a stag bounding over the mountains, is not clear. Either way she means the metaphor, however, the message is quite the same: All through the night, until the darkness turns to light and the morning breeze signals the beginning of a new day,[3] she invites him to enjoy all the delights she can offer him.

Whether or not her metaphors of "lilies" and "rugged mountains" are meant to apply to specific parts of her body or to her body generally as a place for her lover to enjoy is debatable. In 4:5 the woman's breasts are compared to twin gazelles "that feed among the lilies," and in 5:13 the man's lips are called lilies. "Lily" is a common metaphor in the Song of Songs, and the meaning varies with the use,[4] but it always signifies something delightful. On the other hand, the phrase translated "rugged mountains" by the R.S.V. in 2:17 is literally the "cleft," or "split," mountains and could be a reference to the woman's breasts and the cleavage between them.[5] If so, she is specifically inviting her lover to fondle her breasts. Yet even if this is not the specifically intended meaning of "cleft mountains," an invitation to fondle her would certainly be included in the broader sense of her reply. To his request for lovemaking she responds with loving affirmation. He belongs to her, and she belongs to him (2:16), and to them belong the delights of intimate contact with each other.

The Song is not merely open to the possibility of appreciating physical beauty and mutual longing, desire, and fulfillment; it devotes virtually its entire contents to these matters. What does one do with such open eroticism in Scripture? Unfortunately many people down through the centuries have allegorized the Song and thereby removed what some would view as offensive. By assigning "spiritual meanings" to the obviously erotic statements, they transformed this document and caused it to affirm any one of an amazing number of widely varying belief systems. As a matter of fact, for centuries allegorical interpretation of the Song prevailed as the dominant method of exposition by both Jews and Christians.

Various passages in the Old Testament employ the imagery of Israel as the wife of God,[6] and many Jewish people have seen in the Song an allegory of God's love for Israel. On the other hand, because of passages such as Revelation 19:7–9; 21:2–4, 9; 22:17, which speak of the Church as the bride of Christ, Christians have tended to interpret the Song as a description of the love between Christ and the Church. And, of course, there have been many variations of and departures from these two allegorical approaches. Medieval Christian scholastics, for example, saw in the Song the marriage between the active and passive aspects of the human intellect. Others have even identified the woman in the Song with the personified Wisdom of Proverbs 8. So varied have been the approaches to and interpretations of the Song of Songs that Marvin Pope, in his massive commentary on this biblical text, devotes 140 pages to summarizing them.[7]

There are some biblical scholars who still endorse allegorical interpretation of the Song, but their number is dwindling toward extinction. Although the frankness of the Song's sexual allusions remains a source of concern for some Jews and Christians, many presently allow the vividness and vitality of its celebration of the joys of human love to express what they were originally meant to communicate. Nevertheless, this does not stop people from wondering why a collection of love poetry was ever included in Scripture.

The Song was included in the Septuagint, the Greek translation of the Hebrew Scriptures, so we know that it was considered part of the sacred collection before the first century A.D. Yet, at Jamnia in A.D. 90, rabbis openly debated whether or not the acceptance of both Ecclesiastes and the Song into the holy writings was proper. Our knowledge of this debate is limited to a few brief statements in rabbinic literature; and these texts reveal that, following arguments for and against inclusion, the participants decided in favor of both Ecclesiastes and the Song. From this debate comes the now-famous pronouncement of Rabbi Akiba: "The whole world is not worth the day on which the Song of Songs was given to Israel, for all the Scriptures are holy, but the Song of Songs is the Holy of Holies."[8] Presumably because of his high regard for the Song, Akiba elsewhere strictly forbids using it in a secular manner in places like a banquet hall (presumably under the influence of a little too much wine).[9] This would indicate that there was some problem with common people who did not read it allegorically!

Perhaps the allegorical interpretation of the Song by rabbis in the first century was a result of its status as sacred Scripture, and allegory was therefore deemed the proper approach worthy of the document. Or perhaps the rabbis affirmed the canonical status of the Song because they had for some time interpreted it allegorically. The fact is that allegory was "in the air" during the first century, and many books on a variety of subjects were interpreted by this method. We may only assert with some confidence that the Song was part of Scripture prior to the application of allegory to its contents by Jewish rabbis. For the most part, Christians adopted from their Jewish heritage both the canonical status of the Song and an allegorical approach to interpreting it.

Egyptian Love Poetry and the Song of Songs

Allegorizing the Song did remove for centuries the problem of asking why such a document was in Scripture, but the advent of thoroughgoing historical analysis of the Bible made allegory more and more impos-

sible to maintain. As scholars began to discover erotic poetry written by members of ancient cultures in the countries that surrounded Israel, they became more aware of the fact that the poems comprising the Song were not at all unique in antiquity.

Perhaps the closest parallels come from various collections of poetry discovered in Egypt, documents that reflect so many similarities to the Song that they have been extremely helpful in increasing our understanding of its structure and meaning. John B. White has demonstrated that these Egyptian collections are composed of individual poems by different authors that were joined together in a somewhat loose fashion, either by catchword association or because they had a unity of theme.[10] In his opinion these poems were produced by an educated class of people who had a fairly high standard of living and ample leisure time. Nevertheless, their poetry was popular in virtually every stratum of Egyptian society, for their poems gave expression to the feelings experienced by people in general.[11] The fantasies of the rich are often the fantasies of the poor as well, and feelings of adoration for one's beloved or love sickness and longing to be near him or her are not the sole possession of any one level of society.

Like the Song of Songs, the Egyptian poems place considerable emphasis upon describing the physical attributes of the beloved and also make frequent references to seeing, hearing, touching, smelling, and fondling.[12] Both the Song and Egyptian poems often describe the setting of lovemaking in rural terms (for example, in a garden or vineyard or forest), and both have their lovers employ the imagery of plants and animals to describe each other,[13] and both describe sexual intercourse in symbolic language. These similarities, which will occasionally be illustrated with specific examples as we study the Song, are very significant. Not only do they provide further concrete reasons for rejecting allegorization of the Song, but they also help us know how to view its structure.

As we read through the Song, we encounter sudden changes of setting, characters, and speakers. One moment we read of fields and sheep and the poem speaks of the beloved as a shepherd; and a moment later we are reading a description of the beloved as a king, and the

surroundings are those of a royal palace. With no transition statements, the poetic imagery as well as the characters who are speaking change with amazing abruptness, and there is no obvious plot line that indicates that the Song is telling a continuous story. Scholars have nevertheless sought to decipher some sort of dramatic story involving specifically definable characters and sequences; and their hypotheses, as ingenious as they are diverse, reveal various degrees of frustrated formulations of imaginary stories.

Attempts to discover a story line in the Song are apparently misguided, for there does not appear to be any sort of continuous story about the joys and trials of a particular couple. As in the collections of Egyptian poetry, the Song seems to be a collection of once-separate poems whose original purpose for composition we cannot discern. Nor can we decipher exactly why they were collected and linked together in their present form. Fortunately, this does not pose a dilemma for our purposes in studying what the Song says about sex. We can interact with the symbolism without worrying about the overall structure. There is no need to struggle to see some elusive story line running through the entire Song, for there is none. We need only seek to understand the meaning of the multitude of images in the poems and enjoy this celebration of the romantic aspects of life.

Flattery as Foreplay: Praising Beauty (Part One)

Frequently in the Song of Songs a man or woman will speak very imaginative praise for the physical beauty of his or her beloved and, from a modern vantage point, some of these descriptive statements appear extremely humorous. What man today would whisper seductively in his wife's ear, "Your teeth are like a flock of shorn ewes that have come up from the washing" (4:2), or "Your nose is like a tower of Lebanon, overlooking Damascus" (7:4)? What woman today would describe her man to other people by saying, "His body is ivory work, encrusted with saphires. His legs are alabaster columns, set upon bases

of gold" (5:14, 15)? What seems amusing to us was very understandable to the author(s) of these poems, however, and upon closer analysis we can appreciate the meaning that underlies these descriptions of beauty.

One lengthy praise of a woman's beauty occurs in 4:1–7. Beginning with a general statement, "Behold you are beautiful, my love, behold you are beautiful!", the man proceeds to extol specific aspects of his lady's appearance, starting with her eyes and moving downward.

> Your eyes are doves
> behind your veil.
> Your hair is like a flock of goats,
> moving down the slopes of Gilead.
>
> *(4:1)*

The precise meaning of his comparison of her flashing dark eyes with doves is not readily apparent. More understandable is the imagery of a herd of the coal black goats of Palestine descending a mountainside, which graphically portrays her long wavy black hair, streaming beautifully onto her shoulders and down her back (cf. 5:11, where the woman says of the man, "his locks are wavy, black as a raven"). In contrast to her jet-black hair, the woman's teeth are sparkling white.

> Your teeth are like a flock of shorn ewes
> that have come up from the washing,
> all of which bear twins,
> and not one of them is bereaved.
>
> *(4:2)*

A similar contrast between a woman's dark hair and white teeth is made in an Egyptian poem, and its meaning is much more readily understandable than the imagery here in the Song: "Blacker is her hair than the blackness of the night. . . . [Whiter (are) her teeth] than flakes of (white) stone at cutting."[14] Yet in spite of the odd-sounding nature of the compliment in the Song 4:2, it actually expresses more than does the Egyptian poem. Before the shepherds sheared the wool

from their sheep, they would wash them, and the Hebrew lover recalls this image as he considers his lady's clean white teeth; but there is yet more to his compliment. Not only are the ewes clean, they are also healthy, as is indicated by the fact that they are all pregnant with twins and give birth to both lambs in healthy condition, an oddity at that time.[15] In other words, the woman's teeth are white and even, and none of them is missing. When she smiles, there is nothing unsightly about her teeth, and they are framed wonderfully by her red lips.

> Your lips are like a scarlet thread,
>   and your mouth is lovely.
> Your cheeks are like halves of a pomegranate
>   behind your veil.

(4:3)

Furthermore, her cheeks blush their color through her semitransparent veil, reminiscent of sliced sections of the highly prized pomegranate. From the man's viewpoint, every aspect of her face is lovely.

Her beauty does not stop with her face, either. As the man gazes upon her body below her veil he states,

> Your neck is like the tower of David,
>   built for an arsenal,
> whereupon hang a thousand bucklers,
>   all of them shields of warriors.

(4:4)

At first glance this description would seem to be even more bizarre than the rest. What sort of visual image pertaining to female beauty could he possibly have in mind when comparing her neck to a fortress displaying instruments of war? A great many conjectures have been made concerning this verse, as you may well imagine. Perhaps the most plausible explanation is that she wore a rather large and ornate necklace. Consequently, when he looked at her neck, which not only was held straight, keeping her head erect and in a noble-looking posture, but also supported a bespangled necklace, he was reminded of the

tower of David, a symbol of national strength and pride. She had, in effect, a noble bearing.

The man is not embarrassed about praising parts of her anatomy other than her neck and head. Allowing his gaze to go lower, he says,

> Your breasts are like two fawns,
>   twins of a gazelle,
>   that feed among the lilies.
>
>   *(4:5)*

In Arabian writings the gazelle was praised for its beauty and perfect form;[16] and by using this animal to describe his lover's breasts, the man is commenting that they are a beautifully matched pair—twins. Perfectly shaped, they enhance the total picture of her beauty. Furthermore, the man's next comment reveals that he intends to enjoy doing more than merely observing her beautiful breasts:

> Until the day breathes
>   and the shadows flee,
> I will hie me to the mountain of myrrh
>   and the hill of frankincense.
>
>   *(4:6)*

Employing the same phrase used by the woman in 2:17 to invite her lover to come and enjoy sexual union with her, he affirms his intent to make love with her throughout the night. Only here, instead of calling her breasts "cleft mountains" as in 2:17, he compares them to a mountain of spices, a fragrant and delightful place on which to play until the new day dawns.

After stating his intention, the man woos his lady much as the lover in 2:10–15 asked his loved one to come out of her place of hiding. Instead of comparing her, as before, to a dove hiding in a cliff, however, he likens her place of refuge to the remote places in the mountains north of Palestine where the lions and leopards make their dens. He wants her to leave her place of seclusion and join him "until the day breathes and the shadows flee."

Praising the beauty of the beloved is an activity of both men and women in the Song, although the women's use of such praise is not employed as a means of initiating lovemaking. This does not mean that the Song never describes a woman taking the initiative to woo the man, as 3:1–4 clearly reveals. Yet when the woman praises her man in 5:10–16, she is speaking to a group of women, not to her beloved; and her poetically symbolic language is for the purpose of impressing them, not for stimulating him. She begins her verbal portrait with a general statement, "My beloved is all radiant and ruddy, distinguished among ten thousand" (5:10), and then gives a head-to-toe description. Stating that his head is fine gold and his wavy hair is as black as a raven, she proceeds to say, "His eyes are like doves beside springs of water, bathed in milk, fitly set" (5:12). Evidently she means that the dark irises of his eyes, beautifully set in their white-colored eyeballs, remind her of the way doves like to bathe in water. Then she compares her love's cheeks to sweet-smelling beds of spices and his lips to the fragrance of liquid myrrh. So wonderful is he in her eyes that she asserts his priceless value by saying, "His legs are alabaster columns, set upon bases of gold. His appearance is like Lebanon, choice as the cedars" (5:15). In short, he is the picture of strength and beauty from head to foot; and not only is he a "good looker," but he is also a sweet talker: "His speech is most sweet, and he is altogether desirable"(5:16).[17]

There are several more instances in the Song of Songs where detailed descriptions of beauty are given, and we will presently turn to them. Before doing so, though, we should be aware that ancient Egyptian love poetry also contained similar material. Note how the Egyptian poet in the following selection, after a general statement of beauty, praises a particular woman by beginning with her eyes and working his way downward to her feet:

> Unique is a sister, without her duplicate,
> (who is) more beautiful than any woman.
> See, she is like the Star Goddess rising,
> at the beginning of a favorable year.
> (She is) an excellent one who is bright,
> who is shining of skin,

who is beautiful of eyes which stare.
Her lips, which speak, are sweet.
She has not a word too much.
One high of neck, one bright of nipples,
real lapis-lazuli is her hair.
Her arms excel gold;
her fingers are like lotus flowers.
One drooping of buttocks, one slim-waisted,
her thighs extend her perfection.
Her step is pleasing when she treads upon the earth.
She seizes my heart with her embrace.
She causes that the necks of all men
turn back at the sight of her.[18]

Since this poem reflects an Egyptian concept of female beauty, the imagery is somewhat different from that which we find in similar Hebrew descriptions in the Song. The poet calls attention to the wide-eyed, staring appearance of the woman's eyes, a characteristic often portrayed in ancient Egyptian artwork. We might also conclude that a highly praised quality for women was that they avoided talking too much, for the poet lists this commendable attribute along with her physical traits. On the precise meaning of "drooping buttocks" we may only speculate, but one thing is clear: The woman is so lovely that men turn their heads to watch her as she walks by. Such a beautiful creature is she that the poet, who calls her "sister," likens her to a goddess. The term *sister* is a term of endearment found frequently in Egyptian poetry, the Song of Songs, and elsewhere in ancient literature[19] and has no kinship connotation. A man would call his lover "my sister," and a woman would call her beloved "my brother."

Flattery as Foreplay: Praising Beauty (Part Two)

Returning from Egyptian poems to the Song, we notice a variation of the motif of a man praising his lady from top to bottom. In 7:1–13 the man praises his lady by beginning with her feet and proceeding upward

to her head; but here as well as in 4:1–8, the purpose for his flattery again functions as a sort of foreplay.

> How graceful are your feet in sandals,
>   O queenly maiden!
> Your rounded thighs are like jewels,
>   the work of a master hand.

(7:1)

Concerning the woman's feet, Marvin Pope comments, "The sandal left the top of the foot virtually bare and this was apparently regarded as especially captivating."[20] He points out that in Judith, a book in the Old Testament Apocrypha, when Judith prepared herself in an attractive manner in order to seduce and then to kill Holofernes, the general of the Babylonian king Nebuchadnezzar, the story says, "Her sandal ravished his eyes" (Judith 16:9). Thus, our man in the Song of Songs is excited as he observes his woman's graceful feet; and moving his gaze upward, he adds that her nicely curved thighs are like the beautiful work of a master artist. She is like a well-proportioned statue; even her stomach is worthy of praise.

> Your navel is a rounded bowl
>   that never lacks mixed wine.
> Your belly is a heap of wheat,
>   encircled with lilies.

(7:2)

A number of the words in the Song are difficult to decipher, and the meaning of the term translated "navel" in verse 2 (verse 3 in the Hebrew text) by the R.S.V. is obscure.[21] Most scholars believe that in this context it either means "vulva" or "navel." If the term means "navel," then perhaps the poet is associating her belly button with feasting imagery. In antiquity people nearly always mixed their wine with water (that is, mixed wine), and so the man would be commenting on the intoxicating things which her navel holds for him, for its hollow shape reminds him of a drinking glass. On the other hand, since

the progression is from feet to head in this poem, and no other body part receives two descriptive sentences, some scholars believe that between *thighs* (7:1b) and *belly* (7:2b) the poet mentions the woman's vulva. If such be the case, then 7:2a is a metaphor for her vulva, which is like a wine bowl at a festival, a receptacle for that which is delightfully intoxicating.[22] Verse 2b is even more difficult to understand, for there the man proceeds to compare her belly to a round heap of wheat surrounded by white flowers, an obscure image which is very puzzling.

From her belly he moves up to her breasts, repeating the same metaphor used in 4:5: "Your two breasts are like two fawns, twins of a gazelle" (7:3). And again he speaks of the neck as that which is strong and noble, holding the head erect: "Your neck is like an ivory tower" (7:4a). The staggering wealth that would be required to construct a tower out of ivory reveals the magnitude of the compliment. Her neck is priceless, and the head it supports is equally as valuable.

> Your eyes are pools in Heshbon,
>   by the gate of Bathrabbim.
> Your nose is like a tower of Lebanon,
>   overlooking Damascus.
> Your head crowns you like Carmel,
>   and your flowing locks are like purple;
> a king is held captive in the tresses.
>
> *(7:4b–5)*

From a contemporary Western cultural perspective, there is little problem with appreciating the poetic imagery of comparing her eyes to pools of water, but the comparison of her nose to a lookout tower seems curious, to say the least! Perhaps the man thinks that a long, straight nose is very beautiful, or perhaps he here intends the Hebrew term *'ap*, which normally means "nose," to signify her whole face. The word *'ap* is used for "face" in various places in the Old Testament, but when so used, it is always in the plural form and occurs all but once in a phrase describing the action of bowing down with one's face to the ground.[23] The one use where the meaning is different is where Adam is told, "In

the sweat of your face *('appe'ka)* you shall eat bread" (Genesis 3:19). In spite of the linguistic problems involved, some scholars still insist that *'āp* in Song 7:4 refers to the woman's face.[24] If they are correct, then the imagery probably indicates that the woman's face, with her "pool eyes," sits atop a magnificent neck and has an ever-watchful gaze symbolized by a watchtower.[25] Linguistically, however, the evidence points more in the direction of translating the singular *'āp* in 7:4c with the same meaning as in 7:8c (literally "breath of your nose") and concluding that the poet views a long, straight nose as very attractive.

Regardless of whether we translate *'āp* "nose" or "face," we can be assured that the poet's original intention was to be complimentary. Like the lofty and fully forested Mount Carmel, her head is held high and is covered with long, luxuriant hair. There is even a royal quality about her appearance, for he compares her flowing hair to the royal color purple. So lovely are her long tresses that she could hold a king captivated in them.

There is an obvious motivation for the man's flattering description of his lady, for no sooner does he finish his praise of her than he states his intention to enjoy her beauty. Comparing her breasts to clusters of dates on a date palm tree, he makes known his desire to climb the tree and take hold of the clusters (7:6–8a). This symbolic way of saying that he wishes to fondle her breasts is then expanded by the addition of three further similes. With an expression of desire to enjoy her sweetness, he says with some longing, "Oh, may your breasts be like clusters of the vine" (7:8b). Then, he adds that the sweet scent of her breath is like apples and her kisses are like the best wine he has ever tasted (7:8c–9).

Such generous praise is not without effect, for she responds to his advances with a warm invitation to come and enjoy her. Acknowledging that she belongs to him and that he desires her, the woman tenderly says, "Come, my beloved"; and then, continuing his use of fruit imagery to describe their lovemaking, she invites him to the vineyard (7:10–12). In an idyllic garden filled with sweet smells and the tastes of luscious fruit, she promises,

There I will give you my love.
The mandrakes give forth fragrance,
   and over our doors are all choice fruits,
new as well as old,
   which I have laid up for you, O my beloved.

(7:12c–13)

Several factors reveal that this is certainly not the first time this loving couple has experienced the sweet fruit of lovemaking. The man, for example, already has an intimate knowledge of her body (7:1–5); and he is extremely forthright in telling her of his intentions to fondle her breasts (7:7–8). Furthermore, the woman alludes to their past experiences when she speaks of "choice fruits, new as well as old." She is promising that there will be new and fresh aspects to their love as well as repetition of the delights already experienced. They have been married for a while, but for them the honeymoon is not over. As they continue to love each other, their mutual enjoyment continues to blossom like the sweet fruit of Palestine.

A Virgin Bride on Her Wedding Night

Song of Songs 4:9–5:3 describes the first sexual encounter of a young couple on their wedding night. Unlike the experienced couple in 7:1–13, the bride and groom are looking forward to an exciting *new* experience. Although the language of love used by the newlyweds also employs metaphors of fruits and spices, and the sequence of events is similar to those in 7:1–13, with the husband flattering his new bride in 4:9–15, his words lack the intimate knowledge displayed in the man's praise of his wife's body in 7:1–5. Here the young man is indeed thrilled with his bride, but much of the thrill for him is due to his anticipation of discovery.

As he gazes into the eyes of his new wife, he is rather overwhelmed by her nearness.

You have ravished my heart, my sister, my bride,
    you have ravished my heart with a glance of your eyes,
    with one jewel of your necklace.
How sweet is your love, my sister, my bride!
    how much better is your love than wine,
    and the fragrance of your oils than any spice!

                      (4:9–10)

Employing the term of endearment "my sister," which we noted earlier in Egyptian poetry, he proclaims that he is so enamored with her that even the sight of her necklace stimulates him. He is, undoubtedly, *excited*!

By appealing to his senses of sight, taste, and smell, the groom tells his bride how much he adores her. The smell of her perfume is sweeter than anything imaginable, and her love is far better than his favorite wine. She is like a wonderful garden filled with sweet fragrances to be smelled and tasty fruits to be eaten.

Your lips distil nectar, my bride;
    honey and milk are under your tongue:
    the sent of your garments is like the scent of Lebanon.
A garden locked is my sister, my bride,
    a garden locked, a fountain sealed.
Your shoots are an orchard of pomegranates
    with all choicest fruits,
    henna with nard,
nard and saffron, calamus and cinnamon,
    with all trees of frankincense,
myrrh and aloes,
    with all chief spices—
a garden fountain, a well of living water,
    and flowing streams from Lebanon.

                      (4:11–15)

She is a virgin bride dressed beautifully for her marriage, and her clothes have been scented liberally with various perfumes. Her new husband describes her virginity with the metaphors of a locked garden and a sealed fountain, images that portray the protected nature of her

body. In ancient Palestine it was not uncommon for vineyards, orchards, and gardens to be surrounded by rock walls or thick hedges of thornbushes, which protected the fruit from intruders.[26] Like a guarded garden containing many tasty fruits that no one had hitherto enjoyed because the gate leading into it was locked, the virgin bride is as yet untouched. She is also like a spring of cool water, so precious in the arid climate of Palestine, where water is a limited commodity. But this spring has been sealed so that no one could benefit from its life-giving coolness.

Now all this will change. With great anticipation the groom announces his desire to enter the garden and taste the fruits and drink from the fountain. Whereas before his bride was a sealed fountain, now she will become for him like a well of living water and a stream flowing from the mountains of Lebanon. In the Old Testament flowing water is frequently called "living water," to distinguish it from the still water found, for example, in a pond. Typically cooler and lacking any sort of stagnation, flowing water is generally more desirable than still water; and the new bride is very desirable. Whereas before her garden was locked, protecting all her choice fruits, now the rightful owner has come to unlock the gate and partake of her delights.

The groom likens his bride's kisses to the sweet nectar of flowers, and his reference to honey and milk under her tongue (4:11) is probably an allusion to the lingering sweet taste left in his mouth after kissing her. In several other Old Testament passages, the expression of holding something under the tongue indicates an attempt to prolong the pleasure of its taste by savoring it.[27] Such is certainly the intention of the groom, who longs to savor such delightful fruits in his new bride's garden.

In reply, the bride continues the groom's garden imagery as she warmly responds to his advances. Far from revealing any hesitation or resistance, she invites him to come and enjoy all that she has to offer.

> Awake, O north wind,
>   and come, O south wind!
> Blow upon my garden,
>   let its fragrance be wafted abroad.

> Let my beloved come to his garden,
> and enjoy its choicest fruits.

(4:16)

The sexual nature of her words is clearly evident as she invites the winds to blow the smell of her perfume toward her beloved and further excite his passion. She *wants* him to consummate the marriage; and of course, he is *ready*.

> I come to my garden, my sister, my bride,
> I gather my myrrh with my spice,
> I eat my honeycomb with my honey,
> I drink my wine with my milk.

(5:1)

In response to her invitation, the groom employs four different verbs to describe his actions: "I come . . . I gather . . . I eat . . . I drink." He narrates his consummation of the marriage as the full enjoyment of his garden, but this imagery is not sufficient. Alluding also to the metaphors of wine, honey, and milk from 4:10–11, he indicates that his bride is to him all the combined delicacies imaginable.

As the wedding-night poem of 4:9–5:1 concludes with the newly-weds enmeshed in lovemaking, yet another voice is heard in the poem. The final words belong neither to the bride nor to the groom but to a third party, who speaks to the loving couple.

> Eat, O friends, and drink:
> drink deeply, O lovers!

(5:1e)

The identity of this third voice that encourages the lovers to enjoy each other fully has posed problems to many people while reading this particular poem, but such concern to assign an identity to the voice is unnecessary. The presence of an anonymous speaker who addresses one or both lovers is not an uncommon feature of ancient love poetry. Poets simply used this form of anonymous address to speak encouragement to the lovers whom they portrayed in their poems.[28]

Although most of the poetry in the Song is written in the first person, presenting the direct speech of the man or woman, in Egyptian poetry there are numerous places where the poet speaks to one or both of the lovers. Often the sexual imagery employed in these instances is far more explicit than that used in the Song. Compare, for example, the delicate encouragement in 5:1e for the lovers to eat and drink deeply with the following selections from Egyptian works:

> You may bring it to the house of the sister
> when you pant after her cave. . . .
> Thus she will tell you:
> "Take me in your embrace.
> When the day dawns, we will be likewise."[29]

> May you bring it (into) the hall of the sister,
> you alone, without another.
> You can accomplish your desire in her thicket.
> The halls shall be whirling.
> The heavens pant with storms.
> . . . she may bring you her fragrance,
> an odor which overflows to cause
> those who are present to become intoxicated.[30]

In these directions the poet employs some of the same imagery of the sweet smell of the woman and the intoxicating nature of loving her that the Song uses, but the sexual nature of the language in the Egyptian poems is anything but subtle. In fact, it borders on being rather crude.

Humor in the Song of Songs

Parts of the Song were written to be humorous, as may be seen especially in 5:2–6:3. The whole poem is a spoof—a playful drama describing the woman's supposed painful loss of her beloved. Yet there is more than just humor involved in this poem. It represents a bittersweet type of humor with a moral, addressing the serious dimension of losing one's beloved through doing something foolish. Narrated by the woman, the poem begins with a description of how her beloved knocked upon her

door while she lay asleep in her bed. In loving words he asked her to open the door for him, but she hesitated for a little while, considering the bother it would be to get out of bed and go to the door.

> I had put off my garment,
>> how could I put it on?
> I had bathed my feet,
>> how could I soil them?

(5:3)

Her hesitation proved disastrous; for when she failed to respond, her beloved was offended and left. Before his departure she realized that the minor inconveniences of putting on her clothes and dirtying her feet in walking to the door were of little consequence, but her decision came too late. Now that she realized how much she wanted him, he had gone.

> My beloved put his hand to the latch,
>> and my heart was thrilled within me.
> I arose to open to my beloved,
>> and my hands dripped with myrrh,
> my fingers with liquid myrrh,
>> upon the handles of the bolt.
> I opened to my beloved,
>> but my beloved had turned and gone.

(5:4–6a)

Whereas before she did not want to soil her feet to open the door, now she frantically runs about through the city searching for her beloved. Experiencing considerable agony in her search, she wails in lament to a supposed audience:

> I adjure you, O daughters of Jerusalem,
>> if you find my beloved,
> that you tell him
>> I am sick with love.

(5:8)

In response to her plea, the daughters of Jerusalem ask why her beloved is so special that she should make such a commotion about his absence. The woman is very willing to sing the praises of her man and paint the majestic mental image of his physical beauty we considered previously (5:10–16).

In 6:1 the daughters of Jerusalem are convinced of the great value of the lady's lover, and they ask her which way he went so that they might help her to find him. At this point we discover that the whole episode is only a joke, for the woman replies,

> My beloved has gone down to his garden,
>   to the beds of spices,
> to pasture his flock in the gardens,
>   and to gather lilies.
> I am my beloved's and my beloved is mine;
>   he pastures his flock among the lilies.
>
> *(6:2–3)*

Employing the garden imagery that we have seen elsewhere describing the sweetness of lovemaking (for example, 4:12–5:1; 7:6–13), she informs us that her beloved is in bed with her, enjoying his garden. The whole poem is a playful way of allowing the woman to recite for others how wonderfully handsome and lovable is her man, and it reveals the foolishness of losing such a priceless treasure through an inconsiderate and selfish action.

We also find amusing material in Egyptian love poetry, although the joking tends to be somewhat coarse.

> If you seek to handle
> my thighs together with my breasts . . .,
> (would) you leave when you remember food?
> Are you a gluttonous man?
> (Would) you . . . [go] because of clothes?
> I am a possessor of sheets.
> (Would) you go because of hunger?
> Take my breasts.
> Abundant for you is their offering.[31]

While the imagery and the language of love in the Song is at times playful and certainly celebrates the full enjoyment of sexual love, the poetry does not exhibit the tendency of this Egyptian example toward the sort of humor we would expect in a barroom. The Song is erotic— of this fact there should be no doubt—but it is not crude in its eroticism. Celebrating the joys of love in an open manner, it nevertheless does so in a way that, in spire of its candidness, should not at all be an embarrassment to those who study sexuality in the Bible.

Conclusions

The Song merely gives full expression to the viewpoint we have seen in Deuteronomy and Proverbs: Sexual intercourse is a wholesome and enjoyable part of the marriage relationship and should be a source of joy for both husband and wife. From the perspective of the community of faith (men and women seeking to live obedient lives of faithfulness to their God), the Song provides evidence of divine blessing upon enjoying the sensuous dimensions of life. God himself created men and women as sexual beings and gave sensual pleasures to be enjoyed fully. Thus, the totally unembarrassed expressions of desire in the Song are incorporated into the Scriptures as an affirmation of the body—we are physical creatures with valid emotions of love and passion. God is not anxious about sex; he created it!

Notes

1. In the Song 8:6 there is a statement that "love is strong as death," and it is possible to see in this a religious affirmation that sexual love, and the resulting procreation of new life, is the way that life triumphs over death. Viewed in this way, 8:6 could provide a religious foundation for the Song as a whole, in that sex provides the answer to every person's fate of going to Sheol at death (see the description of Sheol in the previous chapter on Proverbs). Yet this interpretation is very questionable. Although it is true that having children was viewed by the ancient Hebrews as the way a man lived on in his

children (see the chapter on Deuteronomy), it is doubtful that the Song is concerned with this issue. The strength of love in 8:6–7 is merely an intensifying of the descriptions of passion revealed throughout the Song. Verse 6 gives the positive dimension of love, and verse 7 gives the dark side of love: "Jealousy is cruel as the grave."

2. Marvin Pope, *Song of Songs*, the Anchor Bible (Garden City, N.Y.: Doubleday & Company, Inc., 1977), pp. 399–400, gives information concerning doves in the literature of antiquity as well as the use of doves in the cultic rituals of various cultures.

3. Shortly before dawn a sea breeze typically blows over Palestine. See Morris Jastrow, Jr., *The Song of Songs, Being a Collection of Love Lyrics of Ancient Palestine* (Philadelphia: J. B. Lippincott, 1921), p. 190.

4. "Lily" is used in 2:1, 2, 16; 4:5; 5:13; 6:2, 3.

5. Cf. 8:10, where the woman likens her breasts to towers.

6. E.g., Isaiah 54:5–7; 62:4–5; Hosea 2:16, 19–20.

7. Pope, *Song of Songs*, pp. 89–229.

8. Mishnah, *Yadayim* 3:5.

9. Tosefta, *Sanhedrin* 12:10; cf. *TB Sanhedrin* 101a.

10. John B. White, *A Study of the Language of Love in the Song of Songs and Ancient Egyptian Poetry*, Society of Biblical Literature Dissertation Series (Missoula, Mont.: Scholars Press, 1978), pp. 80–81.

11. Ibid., pp. 79, 82.

12. Ibid., pp. 99–103.

13. Ibid., pp. 108–9, 118.

14. Translation by John White, Ibid., pp. 189–90. From the Louvre C 100 Love Song.

15. Pope, *Song of Songs*, p. 462.

16. Ibid., p. 470.

17. The Hebrew word translated "speech" in the R.S.V. is *ḥēk*, which literally means "the roof of a person's mouth or gums." Sometimes it is used figuratively for "speech" (Prov. 5:3; 8:7; Job 31:30; 33:2) and other times for "taste" (e.g., Job 12:11; 34:3; Prov. 24:13; Song 2:3). If the meaning here in the Song 5:16 is "taste," then the woman is probably speaking about her lover's sweet kisses instead of his sweet speech. See Francis Brown, S. R. Driver, and Charles A. Briggs, *A Hebrew and English Lexicon of the Old Testament* (Oxford, Eng.: Clarendon Press, 1951), p. 335.

18. Translation from the first stanza of the Chester Beatty Love Songs by White, *Language of Love*, pp. 177–78. For more information on other ancient poems in praise of beauty, see J. C. Cooper, "New Cuneiform Parallels to the Song of Songs," *Journal of Biblical Literature* 90 (1971): 157–62.

19. E.g., in Tobit 5:20, Tobit calls his wife "my sister," in Tobit 7:16 Raguel calls his wife "sister," and in Tobit 8:4, 7 Tobias calls his new bride "sister."

20. Pope, *Song of Songs*, p. 614.

21. See Brown, et al., *Hebrew and English Lexicon*, p. 1,057, for cognate terms from other Semitic languages.

22. Pope, *Song of Songs*, p. 617, comments, "Since the movement of the description of the lady's charms is from the feet upward, the locus of the evermoist receptacle between the thighs and the belly would seem to favor the lower aperture." See also Marcia Falk, *Love Lyrics from the Bible: A Translation and Literary Study of the Song of Songs* (London: The Almond Press, 1982), pp. 127–28.

23. Genesis 19:1; 42:6; 48:12; Numbers 22:31; 1 Samuel 24:8(9); 25:23, 41; 28:14; 2 Samuel 14:4, 33; 18:28 et al.

24. E.g., Falk, *Love Lyrics from the Bible*, p. 127.

25. Pope, *Song of Songs*, pp. 626–27, believes that "tower of Lebanon" in 7:4 refers to an actual mountain, not to a man-made tower on top of a mountain.

26. Numbers 22:24 and Psalm 80:12 speak of a vineyard protected by a rock wall, and Proverbs 24:31 mentions a hedge of thorn plants. Isaiah 5:5 speaks of a combination rock wall and thorny hedge. For a much later parallel, see Jesus' parable of the man who planted a vineyard and built a wall around it (Mark 12:1–9).

27. Psalm 10:7; Job 20:12. See Pope, *Song of Songs*, p. 486.

28. See White, *The Language of Love*, pp. 92–95, 129–30.

29. Translation of the Nakht-Sobek Cycle of P. Chester Beatty I, first stanza, by White, ibid., p. 183.

30. Ibid., second stanza.

31. Love Songs of Papyrus Harris 500, poem one, translated by White, ibid., p. 169.

The Gospels: Jesus' Teaching on Radical Love and Moral Purity

5

When we move from the sensuous love poetry of the Song of Songs to the New Testament stories about Jesus, a considerable transition occurs. Whereas the Song of Songs is wholly devoted to celebrating human love, there is little in the Gospels that pertains to sexuality. Sexual matters, although not absent from this material, are in no way a major concern. Nevertheless, in the few Gospel stories that address sexual problems, enough information exists to show that the teaching of Jesus contains some rather fundamental differences from the mainstream of Jewish thinking during his time. This is especially evident in the case of divorce, a topic to be discussed at length in this chapter, but is also apparent in other aspects of Jesus' thought.

Jesus' statements pertaining to sexuality reveal an amazing combination of forceful demands for complete purity and gentle treatment of those who were guilty of sexual offenses. On the one hand he commanded a moral purity that exceeded the rigorous demands of most of the religious leaders of his day. On the other hand he exhibited a

forgiving attitude toward the riffraff of his society that shocked and offended many of his contemporaries. Although his warm acceptance of people won great popularity for him among the common populace, Jesus' behavior aroused fierce opposition from some of the religious leaders. He acknowledges in Matthew 11:19, for example, that some accuse him of being "a gluttonous man, and a drunkard, and a friend of tax-collectors and sinners." This dual role of preaching moral purity and associating with riffraff must be held in tension as one examines Jesus' teaching on sexuality.

A forceful preacher, Jesus frequently employed extreme language in order to make his point. His words were often shocking and tended to have a jolting effect.

> If your right eye causes you to sin, tear it out and throw it away from you. For it is better for you to lose one part of your body than to have your whole body thrown into hell. And if your right hand causes you to sin, chop it off and throw it away from you. For it is better for you to lose one part of your body than to have your whole body thrown into hell.
>
> *(Matt. 5:29–30)*

This drastic assertion occurs in the context of a statement on adultery that begins, "You have heard that it was said, 'Do not commit adultery,' but I say to you that everyone who looks at a woman for the purpose of desiring her has already committed adultery with her in his heart" (Matt. 5:27–28). The grotesque picture of a man tearing an eye out of his head in order to stop himself from looking at a woman and lusting for her is an extremely vivid way of demanding purity in one's thoughts. Graphic words of this nature have a profound impact on people and impress them with the seriousness of the matter under consideration.

Most of the sayings collected in Matt. 5–7 (The Sermon on the Mount) serve as good illustrations of Jesus' intensification of contemporary Jewish ethical standards. Going beyond simple adherence to Old Testament laws, he taught that people should be concerned about their thoughts and the motivation for their actions, not just outward obser-

vance of rules. In Matt. 5:21–26, for example, Jesus deepens the murder prohibition of Deuteronomy 5:17 to include a ban on angry and cruel speech. To live in accordance with Jesus' teaching in Matt. 5–7, one's goodness must be much more than mere obedience to laws. It must consist of a piety that (a) does not injure people by saying harsh things to or about them (5:21–26); (b) views women not as objects of lust (5:27–30); (c) would not terminate a marriage for anything but extreme reasons (5:31–32); (d) exhibits nothing but honesty in business transactions (5:33–37); (e) does not plot retaliation when wronged by someone (5:38–42); (f) loves even one's enemies and prays for them (5:43–48); and so on. For Jesus the proper question to ask is not, therefore, "How much can I do without actually being in violation of this law?" He would say that the question should be, "How can I treat everyone with respect and live my life in honesty, neither manipulating nor abusing others, but caring as much about their needs as I do about my own?"

Concern for Society's Downtrodden

Jesus' attitude of extreme interest in the welfare of other people destroys the common tendency to be unconcerned with those who are lower on the ladder of social status. Although Jesus may not have thrown away this ladder completely, his law of love rendered its rungs too weak to bear the weight of standing over others and not caring about their plight. For women, who for ages had stood on lower rungs of the ladder, vulnerable to divorce and rejection if they were unable to bear children or displeased their husbands, a new sense of importance as individuals emerged from the teaching of this young rabbi. Men who would follow Jesus' commands must abandon looking upon women as objects who provide either pleasure or children. Standing beside men as people whose feelings were important, even if their social standing was not as high, women were given a new dignity in a man's world. Jesus' concern for the downtrodden of society was one of the reasons for his extreme popularity among those who occupied the lower rungs of

society's ladder. It was also one of the reasons why those religious leaders who occupied higher rungs of society looked upon him with a certain degree of contempt and called him "a friend of tax-collectors and sinners."

If the downtrodden experienced from Jesus a wonderful kind of acceptance that transcended their social status, they did not find in him one who made their lives morally or ethically easier. His costly call to a life-style of love clearly involved a death blow to living for oneself. Asserting what at first may appear to be contradictory messages, he affirmed, "You are of great worth as a person," while at the same time proclaiming, "You must be a servant to others!" Following Jesus involved giving up one of the very basic human tendencies upon which dehumanization is built: that other people are valuable only insofar as they fulfill one's own needs and desires.

While it would be wrong to portray Jesus as a crusader for women's rights, since that certainly was not the focus of his ministry, at the same time the consequences of his thinking in the area of sexuality should be realized. Whereas a man under the Deuteronomic law might limit himself to sexual intercourse with his wife alone out of fear for his life, under Jesus' law of love a man would exercise sexual restraint due to a concern not to place his own desire above the welfare of others. Furthermore, because Jesus labeled overt sexual fantasy about a certain person as equivalent to the action of physical intercourse, an individual cannot retreat behind the statement, "I never slept with her—I only thought about it." A virgin in the technical sense might be totally polluted through lust-filled thoughts. Purity must be part of a person's entire mental framework and fundamental approach to life, not just an outward conformity to the minimum required by social laws.

Jesus' teaching on purity of thoughts, although radical, was not unique in ancient Judaism. In the Testament of Issachar 7:2, Issachar states, "Except my wife I have not known any woman. I have never committed fornication by the uplifting of my eyes."[1] Similarly, Sirach 23:2, 4–6 says, "O that whips were set over my thoughts, and the discipline of wisdom over my mind. . . . O Lord, Father and God of my life, do not give me haughty eyes, and remove from me evil desire.

Let neither gluttony nor lust overcome me, and do not surrender me to a shameless soul." First-century Judaism should not be regarded as only concerned with meticulous (legalistic) adherence to Jewish law. Certainly there were Jewish people who did fit this unfortunate stereotype, even as some Christians and Jews today exhibit this same tendency. Many adherents of Judaism in Jesus' time were, however, extremely concerned to love God and their neighbors sacrificially. The apocryphal book of Tobit is a delightful story that provides a picture of how an idealized Jewish man shunned his own welfare for the sake of the downtrodden.

A Controversial Encounter with a Prostitute

Luke 7:36–50 is a vivid illustration of how Jesus, the one who spoke forcefully about sexual purity, responded in loving forgiveness to a sexual offender. This rather shocking story opens with Jesus reclining in Oriental fashion on a couch, eating a meal with some Pharisees. Now the Pharisees were extremely careful to observe strict rules in how they prepared their food and made it a policy not to share meals with those who did not keep similar purity laws. Meticulously they made sure that their pots and pans were ritually purified before food was prepared in them (Mark 7:1–4). So conscious were they of obeying Jewish laws that they tithed even their table spices (for example, Matt. 23:23) and usually refused to eat with non-Pharisees lest they inadvertently eat untithed or improperly prepared food. As a result there was sometimes animosity between the Pharisees and other Jews who did not maintain their standards. At least some Pharisees disdainfully called the non-Pharisees *'am ha-aretz* (Hebrew for "people of the land"), resulting in conflict, as the following quotes from Rabbis Hillel and Akiba vividly illustrate:

> R. Hillel said, "No *'am ha-aretz* is religious." R. Akiba [c. A.D. 132] said, "When I was an *'am ha-aretz* I used to say 'If I could get hold of one of the scholars [that is, Pharisaic scribe] I would bite him like an ass.'

'You mean, like a dog,' said his disciples. 'No,' said Akiba, 'an ass's bite breaks bones.' "[2]

We may well imagine the shock when into a room full of Pharisees reclining at table walked a prostitute, who headed straight for Jesus. Her body convulsing with sobs, she cried so hard that she actually washed Jesus' feet with her tears; and, if that were not enough, she dried them with her disheveled hair. Then, as Jesus' host stared in amazed disgust, she began to kiss his feet and, with those defiled hands that had caressed the bodies of many men, poured expensive perfume purchased by the gain of her illicit trade onto the feet of Jesus. Instead of recoiling from the touch of this woman, Jesus used her as an example of how those who have been forgiven a great deal are far more appreciative and consequently express more love than those who have only a little for which to be forgiven. The one who proclaimed purity even in thoughts then turned to a grief-filled prostitute and tenderly said, "Your sins are forgiven . . . your faith has saved you. Go in peace." And to his very moral Pharisee host, Jesus speaks words of censure for not having received him more graciously into his home. In the Gospel stories the religious leaders never respond very well to Jesus' censure, however. So on a different occasion he bluntly told some of them who refused to repent and follow his teaching, "Truly I say to you that the tax-collectors and prostitutes are entering the Kingdom of God before you" (Matt. 21:31).

Jesus' ministry may be accurately described as conforming to the often-repeated remark "A preacher's job is to comfort the afflicted and afflict the comfortable." In short, he did not merely speak what he considered to be commands that were universal in their application. There is no evidence that he meticulously worked out an alternative law code to replace the one under which the Jews lived. He spoke more like a prophet than a lawgiver, addressing different situations in different ways. This is not to say that Jesus was a thoroughgoing proponent of situation ethics; that would certainly be a distortion. But in order to understand Jesus' message, we should recognize that his ministry was prophetic, not in the sense that he primarily predicted the future, but

in the sense that he forcefully called people to repent of their sin and wholeheartedly embrace the rule of God in their lives.

Is It Lawful to Divorce?

Jesus' self-consciousness of his prophetic mission to proclaim the will of God enabled him to alter radically some of the prevailing opinions of his day. One such opinion was that of divorce. The belief expressed in Deuteronomy, that a man had the right to divorce his wife if he so desired, prevailed as the dominant view during Jesus' lifetime. This may be clearly seen in the Mishnah, a collection of sayings of various rabbis that was compiled about A.D. 200. An entire tractate in the Mishnah, entitled *Gittin*, is devoted to explaining the proper manner in which a man should divorce his wife. Detailing such things as how a man should write and deliver a divorce document to his wife (cf. Deut. 24:1–4), there is nothing in the entire tractate that speaks against divorce.[3] In the last section of this text, the views of two Pharisaic schools are contrasted, and this contrast reveals two dominant ways in which Deut. 24:1–4 was interpreted. The passage reports the school of Shammai as holding the more conservative interpretation, teaching that divorce was permitted only if the wife was guilty of some immoral behavior. The school of Hillel, however, was far more lenient, allowing the husband to divorce his wife for an act as insignificant as spoiling his supper. On the basis of Deut. 24:1 ("if then she finds no favor in his eyes") Rabbi Akiba even said that if a man should find a woman more beautiful than his own wife, he could divorce his wife and marry the more attractive woman.[4] Thus, biblical interpretations varied among the Pharisees, but both schools of thought sanctioned divorce. Although Shammai did not agree that a man could divorce his wife because she burned his supper or because he found a more attractive woman, he did not seek to eliminate the husband's right of divorce.

It is of considerable consequence, therefore, that when asked by some Pharisees for his interpretation of Deut. 24:1–4, Jesus dismisses the man's right to divorce his wife and states that the Deut. 24:1–4 law

was only a concession on God's part to the wickedness of people. Two accounts of this discussion are recorded in the Gospels, and it is very helpful to look at them side by side so that the differences in the way they are narrated may be observed.

Mark 10:2–12

[2]And Pharisees came in order to test him and asked if it is lawful for a man to divorce a woman. [3]And he answered them, "What did Moses *command* you?" [4]And they said, "Moses *allowed* one to write a divorce document and to divorce her." [5]And Jesus said to them, "He wrote this *command* because of your hard heart. [6]But from the beginning of creation he made them male and female. [7]Because of this a man will leave his father and mother and he will be united in marriage to his wife [8]and the two will be one flesh, so that they are no longer two but one flesh. [9]What therefore God has joined together, man must not separate."

[10]And when they were in the house, the disciples asked him about this matter again. [11]And he said to them, "Whoever divorces his wife and marries another commits adultery against her; [12]and if she divorces her husband to marry another, she commits adultery."

Matthew 19:3–12

[3]And Pharisees came to him, testing him and saying, "Is it lawful for a man to divorce his wife *for any reason?*" [4]And he answered, "Have you not read that the Creator from the beginning made them male and female?" [5]And he said, "Because of this a man will leave father and mother and he will be united to his wife, and the two will be one flesh, [6]so that they are no longer two but one flesh. What therefore God has joined together, man must not separate."

[7]And they said to him, "Why therefore did Moses *command* one to give a divorce document and to divorce her?" [8]He said to them, "Moses *allowed* you to divorce your wives because of your hard heart, but from the beginning it was not like this. [9]And I say to you that whoever divorces his wife except for fornication and marries another commits adultery."

[10]His disciples said to him, "If such is the relationship of a man with a woman, it is not advantageous to marry." [11]And he said to them, "Not everyone

can accept [or understand] this word, but [only] those to whom it has been given. [12]For there are those who were born eunuchs from their mother's womb, and there are those who were made eunuchs by men, and there are those who have made themselves eunuchs because of the kingdom of heaven. The one who is able to accept [or understand], let him accept [or understand]."

Although these two accounts of the same story essentially communicate equivalent points about marriage and divorce, close comparison of the stories reveals a number of differences. Their beginning statements are similar, but Matt. 19:3 adds a qualifying clause that alters the nature of the Pharisees' question. In Mark 10:2 they ask if divorce itself is lawful, but in Matt. 19:3 legality of divorce is assumed, and the question concerns legitimate reasons for divorce. Next, in Mark 10:3–7, Jesus begins by asking what the law "commands," and the Pharisees respond that Moses "allowed" divorce. To this Jesus answers that Moses gave this "command" only because of "your hard heart," and he justifies this viewpoint by appealing to the creation account in Genesis 2:24. However, this part of the story in Matthew occurs not after the opening statement but in verses 7–8, *after* an explanation of how God intended marriage to be from the beginning (verses 4–6). Not only is the discussion arranged differently, but the wording is altered significantly. Whereas in Mark 10:3–4 Jesus asks what Moses "commanded" and the Pharisees respond that Moses "allowed" divorce, in Matt. 19:4–6 Jesus first teaches on Gen. 2:24, the Pharisees respond by asking why Moses "commanded" divorce (19:7), and Jesus then replies that Moses only "allowed" divorce (19:8). Furthermore, Mark 10:10–12 has Jesus' disciples asking him later about his position, and to this group alone he states that the one who initiates divorce (whether the

man or the woman) and remarries is guilty of adultery. Matthew, on the other hand, arranges the conversation so that Jesus speaks an abbreviated version of Mark 10:11 not privately to his own disciples but publicly to the Pharisees, and Mark 10:10 and 12 are deleted entirely. In Matthew's version the information given by Jesus only to his disciples in 19:10–12 has no parallel in Mark.

How do we account for these subtle yet significant differences between the two Gospel stories? Only an extremely abbreviated explanation may be offered here concerning the complicated nature of the literary relationship between the Synoptic Gospels: Matthew, Mark, and Luke.[5] A great amount of detailed analysis of these Gospels has shown that Mark was the first to be written, probably in Rome between A.D. 60 and 70. Mark's story about Jesus was not intended to be a formal historical treatise or even a biography in the usual sense of the term. He says nothing of Jesus' birth or childhood, and nearly half of his sixteen chapters describe the last week of Jesus' life. Mark wrote a proclamation of the significance of Jesus' ministry—what could be called a witness document—for Christians undergoing a period of persecution in Rome.

Although Matthew used Mark's Gospel as one of his sources of information and largely followed the Marcan sequence of events, he had a different purpose in writing and modified his sources according to his purpose. Whereas Mark focused on what Jesus *did* and included little discourse material, Matthew was extremely interested in what Jesus *said*. Writing in a Jewish cultural setting primarily for Jewish Christians,[6] Matthew devoted a great amount of space to recording Jesus' teaching, for a dominant Jewish messianic expectation was that the Messiah would bring a divinely inspired interpretation of their Scriptures.[7] He gathered together the sayings of Jesus into extended discourse sections (for example, Matt. 5–7, the Sermon on the Mount) and portrayed Jesus throughout his Gospel as the authoritative interpreter of the Jewish Scriptures. Furthermore, Matthew sought to intensify the contrast between Jesus and his opponents, the religious leaders, by juxtaposing Jesus' absolute obedience to God and his correct understanding of Scripture with their ignorance of the true meaning of the

sacred books and their failure to obey the will of God. Thus, when Matthew used the divorce story from Mark 10:2–12, he modified the sequence and the wording in order to portray more vividly Jesus' understanding of the true reason for the existence and meaning of the statement on divorce in Deut. 24:1–4 and the Pharisees' ignorance of the same. After Jesus explains the true will of God for marriage from the creation account in 19:4–6, the Pharisees are bewildered (19:7). Essentially they are confused over the seeming contradiction between the creation account and Deut. 24:1–4, and so they ask for an explanation of why Moses "commanded" divorce. Jesus explains in reply that God's will is expressed in Gen. 2:24: Marriage should be permanent. The Mosaic legislation in Deut. 24:1–4 is merely a concession to their hard heart—Moses only "allowed" divorce. Matthew's rendition of the story is therefore enhanced by the way he reversed Mark's use of the terms *command* and *allowed*:

Mark 10:3–5	*Matthew 19:7–8*
And he answered them, "What did Moses command you?" And they said, "Moses allowed one to write a divorce document. . . ." And Jesus said to them, "He wrote this command because. . . ."	And they said to him, "Why therefore did Moses command one to give her a divorce document. . . ?" He said to them, "Moses allowed you to divorce your wives because. . . ."

By using techniques such as this simple reversal of terms, Matthew augmented his picture of Jesus as the authoritative interpreter of Scripture whose teaching Christians should follow obediently.

Matthew's use of Mark clearly does not reflect a desire to reproduce the exact wording of his Marcan source. He was much more interested in modifying the stories in order to fit them coherently into his own narrative framework. One should also realize that because Matthew wrote for Jewish Christians living in a Jewish culture, this further influenced the way in which he modified Mark. For example, he rearranged the sequence of the discussion on divorce so that it conformed more closely to the typical format employed by rabbis when

they debated about Scripture. Thus, Matthew sought to cast the story into a setting that would communicate more effectively to his Jewish audience than Mark's effort to tell the story of Jesus to his predominantly Gentile readers. This recasting of the stories becomes very important in seeking to determine what Jesus said about divorce and how his words were used by the early Christians.

Pastoral Use of Jesus' Divorce Teaching in the New Testament

What was the precise wording of Jesus' original prohibition of divorce? It is impossible to say for sure. The earliest record of this saying is found in 1 Corinthians 7:10–11, which was written about A.D. 55, and the statement contains no exception clause: "And to the rest I command, not I but the Lord, let a woman not be separated [or divorced] from her husband. But if she is separated, let her remain unmarried or be reconciled to her husband. And a man should not divorce his wife." This passage will be fully analyzed in Chapter 6, but for now it is important to notice that the divorce prohibition is absolute and is directed both to women and to men. Nevertheless, as we will see later, Paul proceeds to give an exception to the rule in the verses that follow. In other words, he saw Jesus' word as authoritative, but he also sought to be sensitive in the way he applied it to the situation at Corinth.

Luke 16:18 also contains Jesus' divorce prohibition; but, unlike Mark and Matthew, it does not occur in a discussion. Luke places the statement in a somewhat randomly arranged collection of sayings and words it, "Everyone who divorces his wife and marries another commits adultery, and one who marries a divorced woman commits adultery." This whole statement is directed only to men—nothing is said about the woman either divorcing or committing adultery—and may perhaps reflect the closest approximation of Jesus' original words. In Jesus' Jewish culture the man had the right of divorce, but the woman could only divorce in extreme conditions. These are given in the Mishnah,

tractate *Kethuboth* 7:10, and include the following reasons: If the man has a severe skin disease or a morbid growth in his nose (that is, disfigurations) or if he hauls manure or works in a copper mine (that is, his skin stinks) or if he tans leather. If the woman simply cannot stand these conditions, she may demand that her husband divorce her. Consequently, when Jesus gave his divorce prohibition, he may have directed it only toward men, because, aside from a few cases, the men would be the initiators of divorce.

In Roman society, however, it was both legal and common for women to divorce their husbands.[8] So it is quite likely that Mark added the final statement of his story on divorce—"And if she divorces her husband and marries another, she commits adultery" (Mark 10:12)—in order to make Jesus' command more applicable to the circumstances faced by Christians in Rome. In a similar attempt to apply the prohibition to his Jewish culture, Matthew added the exception clause—"except for fornication" (Matt. 19:9)—in order to allow for the "unseemly thing" (*'erwat dābār*) of Deut. 24:1. (Note that there is no exception clause in Mark. He formulated it as an absolute prohibition.) Since Matthew placed Jesus' discussion into the realm of asking what connotes a legitimate reason for divorce by the addition of "for any reason" in Matt. 19:3, Jesus' answer in 19:9 sides with the conservative Jewish (Shammai) view that divorce is allowable only in extreme cases.

Apparently, Matthew, Mark, and Paul all modified Jesus' words out of a pastoral concern that his commands be understandable to the people for whom they wrote. All three men accepted Jesus' prohibition as authoritative, yet they saw no conflict in creatively applying it to new situations. Taking it as a strong prophetic statement, they evidently saw no need to understand the pronouncement as an inflexible law but as a meaning-filled authoritative guideline for Christians.

Indeed, a close investigation of Matt. 19:3–12 and Mark 10:2–12 reveals that the story contains more of an explanation of the basis of marriage than it does anything else. In response to a question about divorce, Jesus reveals his view of marriage and the will of God. In other words, when asked in Matt. 19:3 to define legitimate reasons for divorce, he refocuses the question onto God's will for marriage. For

Jesus the crucial question should be "What is the most pleasing thing I can do for God?" not "How can I divorce and still be a Christian?" The question one should always ask is, "What is the right thing to do?" never "How much can I get away with?" From Jesus' perspective the will of God for marriage is a one-flesh union that is permanent; anything less than that falls short of God's desire for his people. Jesus makes it clear that divorce is an aberration, and he holds an extremely high view of the sanctity of the marriage relationship. Circumstances can and do arise that are so extreme that divorce becomes necessary; but, as with the forceful statement to "pluck out your eye" to avoid lust, drastic measures should be taken to prevent it.

Celibacy as a Respectable Option

Following this rather lengthy treatment of divorce, only Jesus' statement on celibacy in Matt. 19:10–12 remains to be discussed in this chapter:

> His disciples said to him, "If such is the relationship of a man with a woman, it is not advantageous to marry." And he said to them, "Not everyone can accept [or understand] this word, but [only] those to whom it has been given. For there are those who were born eunuchs from their mother's womb, and there are those who were made eunuchs by men, and there are those who have made themselves eunuchs because of the kingdom of heaven. The one who is able to accept [or understand], let him accept [or understand].

This material is unique to Matthew and presents several difficulties in interpretation. Matthew describes the disciples as amazed at Jesus' divorce prohibition, and they question whether or not it is, therefore, advisable to marry. It is hard to know if Jesus' reply in verse 11 speaks directly to the disciples' phrase in verse 10 ("it is not advantageous to marry") or to the whole of his teaching on marriage and divorce in 19:3–9. If Jesus is referring to 19:3–9, then his saying, "Not everyone can accept this word, but only those to whom it has been given,"

would mean that not everyone would be able to live under his radical exclusion of divorce. The additional information in verse 12 on the three ways a man can be a eunuch [that is, celibate], however, make it more probable that Jesus refers in verse 11 to the word of his disciples in verse 10. Thus, in verse 12 he says that whoever is able to remain celibate should do so, but only if the person is specially gifted in this matter (verse 11).

Within a Jewish cultural context such a statement would be quite radical, because in mainstream Judaism, men were under obligation to marry and produce children so as to fulfill the commission of God in Genesis 1:28: "And God said to them, 'Be fruitful and multiply and fill the earth and subdue it.' " Except for a possible delay for intense study of the Scriptures [Torah], a man was expected to marry by age twenty,[9] so that he could do his part in propagating the covenant people of God. So strong was this belief that a man could be expected to divorce his wife if she could bear him no children after ten years of marriage.

> No man may abstain from keeping the law *Be fruitful and multiply*, unless he already has children: according to the School of Shammai, two sons; according to the School of Hillel, a son and a daughter, for it is written, *Male and female created he them*. If he married a woman and lived with her ten years and she bare no child, it is not permitted him to abstain. If he divorced her she may be married to another and the second husband may live with her for ten years. If she had a miscarriage the space [of ten years] is reckoned from the time of the miscarriage. The duty to be fruitful and multiply falls on the man but not on the woman. R. Johanan b. Baroka says: Of them both it is written, *And God blessed them and God said unto them, Be fruitful and multiply*.[10]

In light of this extreme importance placed upon a woman's ability to bear children, we may be somewhat dismayed to learn that, by our standards, when these Jewish women married and began having babies, they were little more than children themselves. When these girls began to menstruate, their fathers soon thereafter would betroth them to a man, which meant that at the tender age of about twelve to thirteen years they were considered mature and were engaged to be married.

The betrothal period lasted one year, after which time the marriage was consummated. Thus, there is a high degree of probability that Mary, the mother of Jesus, was betrothed to Joseph as a mere girl, according to Jewish custom; and Joseph was younger than twenty when they married.[11] Mary would therefore have given birth to Jesus perhaps before she was fourteen years old.

Mary's famous son did not behave according to the expected norms of his society. Since nothing is ever recorded in early Christian literature about Jesus having a wife, even though various statements are made about his family (for example, Mark 3:31; 6:3), nearly all scholars conclude that he never married.[12] There is no indication that he at all diminished the value of the marriage relationship, however. We might note, for example, that both before and after Jesus' statement on celibacy in Matt. 19:11–12, he places high value upon children (18:2–5; 19:13–15). Some groups of Jews did exalt the role of celibacy, primarily in an ascetic quest for total purity. For example, the Essenes who lived at Qumran, the group that produced what have been called the Dead Sea Scrolls, believed that the end of the age was an imminent possibility. In their preparation for this coming catastrophe they practiced celibacy, but this was very much a minority view among the Jews as a whole. There is ample evidence to document that even among some of the Essene groups that lived outside of Qumran the men generally married.[13] Since Matt. 19:11–12 offers no explanation for why celibacy was to be considered an acceptable alternative for Jesus' followers, it is somewhat hazardous to assert the reason that lies behind it. What can be affirmed, however, is that Matt. 19:3–9 espouses a high view of marriage as the will of God and that its purpose goes beyond mere production of offspring. While a Jewish man would be expected to divorce a woman who could bear him no children (Mishnah, *Yebamoth* 6:6), Jesus dismisses divorce for this reason. According to him, God's will is a one-flesh permanent union that is not contingent on production of children. As a matter of fact, even the celibate state, which precludes the possibility of children, is not only acceptable but even seen as a special gift for some in 19:11. The Apostle Paul, himself unmarried, provides an explanation for why celibacy was admirable in

1 Cor. 7, and this passage will supply a much clearer rationale than is available in Matt. 19:10–12.

Conclusions

Several things may be concluded concerning the views of Jesus on sexual matters as they are recorded in the Synoptic Gospels. He not only agreed with the normal Jewish belief that sexual intercourse either before or outside of marriage (that is, fornication) was wrong, but he also asserted that having sexual lust for a particular person is equivalent to committing adultery with that person. Basing his view of the marriage union on the creation story of Genesis 2, he affirmed that God himself is somehow involved in the coming together of man and wife, and therefore the man cannot say that he has the "right" to divorce. Men and women must change their approach to life and seek not merely to obey standards imposed by law but always to seek the best— the will of God. If anything stands in the way of a person attaining God's best in his or her life, that person should take drastic steps to remove the obstacle. And if God has so gifted a person, he or she may remain celibate as a legitimate expression of desire to live fully and completely for God and his kingdom. The single person need not feel uneasy about celibacy nor the married person feel less spiritual for being married. All must come to terms with the radical call of God on their lives and live in the manner God has assigned for them. Sexually speaking, therefore, Jesus taught that God desires sexual intercourse to be limited to one's husband or wife; and basing their marriage on seeking the best for each other, husband and wife should maintain a permanent, one-flesh union.

The Gospel writers sought to interpret this message of Jesus for their own readers in the ways they deemed most appropriate. At times this meant retaining the prophetic power of his assertions unchanged, and at other times it meant making modifications. Thus, early Christian leaders were concerned to take the stories about Jesus and apply them meaningfully to their own situations. They sought to make his

voice a living voice and not reduce him to a great lawgiver of the past. To reduce Jesus to a lawgiver is to diminish the power of his prophetic voice and reduce the radical nature of his message to laws that merely update those found in the Old Testament. As the next chapter reveals, this prophetic nature of Jesus' call was recognized by Paul, who applied it creatively to a terribly perverted notion of freedom in Christ that existed at Corinth.

Notes

1. Trans. R. H. Charles, ed., *The Apocrypha and Pseudepigrapha of the Old Testament in English*, vol. II (Oxford, Eng.: Clarendon Press, 1913).

2. Quote taken from Sherman Elbridge Johnson, *A Commentary on the Gospel According to St. Mark* (London: Adam and Charles Black, 1960), p. 61.

3. There were, of course, some Jewish people who spoke strongly against divorce. For example, Rabbi Eleazar is recorded in Gittin 90b as saying, "If a man divorces his first wife, even the altar sheds tears." [Trans. Maurice Simon, *The Babylonian Talmud, Seder Nashim, Gittin*, vol. II (New York: The Rebecca Bennet Publications Inc., 1959), p. 439.]

4. Gittin 9:10.

5. For a detailed explanation of the literary dependence of Matthew and Luke upon Mark, see Werner Georg Kümmel, *Introduction to the New Testament*, rev. ed., trans. Howard Clark Kee (Nashville: Abingdon Press, 1975), pp. 38–80. A few scholars, such as William R. Farmer, *The Synoptic Problem* (New York: Macmillan, 1964), argue for Matthean priority, but this is definitely a minority position. For personal comparison of passages in the Synoptic Gospels, one should obtain Burton H. Throckmorton, Jr., ed., *Gospel Parallels: A Synopsis of the First Three Gospels* (Nashville, Tenn.: Thomas Nelson Inc., 1967) which arranges parallel Gospel stories beside each other for convenient study.

6. The Jewish nature of Matthew may be seen in a number of ways. For example, whereas Mark occasionally explains the meaning of Jewish customs for his readers, Matthew does not contain such explanatory additions, because they were not needed for his audience (cf. Mark 7:1–5, 11 with Matt. 15:1–2, 5; see also Matt. 5:22; 23:5, 27; 27:6). Matthew is also fond of using Jewish circumlocutions (e.g., "Kingdom of Heaven" is used thirty-three times and "Kingdom of God" occurs only four times, while Mark and Luke nearly always use "Kingdom of God"). Note also the very Jewish setting of the Sermon on

the Mount (Matt. 5–7), especially 6:1–18, which treats the cornerstones of Jewish piety: almsgiving, prayer, and fasting.

7. For a detailed study of Jewish messianic expectation see W. D. Davies, *The Setting of the Sermon on the Mount* (Cambridge, Eng.: Cambridge University Press, 1964), pp. 109–90, esp. pp. 139–90.

8. J. P. V. D. Balsdon, *Roman Women: Their History and Habits* (London: The Bodley Head, Ltd., 1962), pp. 216–17.

9. Mishnah, *Aboth* 5:21; cf. b. Beracoth 6:10.

10. Mishnah, *Yebamoth* 6:6, trans. Herbert Danby, *The Mishnah* (Oxford, Eng.: Oxford University Press, 1933), p. 227.

11. The notion that Joseph was much older than Mary arose later in the Church as an attempt to make the virgin birth of Jesus more credible in response to the attacks of critics. For a fanciful account of Mary's childhood and her eventual marriage to Joseph, an elderly widower, read "The Protevangelium of James," trans. A. J. B. Higgins, in *New Testament Apocrypha*, vol. I, eds. Edgar Hennecke and Wilhelm Schneemelcher, trans. German vol. R. McL. Wilson (Philadelphia: The Westminster Press, 1963), pp. 374–88.

12. William E. Phipps, *Was Jesus Married? The Distortion of Sexuality in the Christian Tradition* (New York: Harper & Row, 1970), is one of the very few who argues that Jesus was married.

13. Josephus, *War* II. 8:13, says that one group of Essenes claimed that failure to marry cut off the prospect of succession and that if all men remained celibate, the human race would be exterminated. The Damascus Document assumes marriage relations (CD V; XVI), and the Messianic Rule permits a man to marry at age twenty (1QSa I).

1 Corinthians: Apostolic Correction of Sexual Aberration

During his life the Apostle Paul was at the center of major controversies; and the legacy we have of his beliefs, as they are represented in the letters he wrote to various churches, continues to spark debates even today. Paul's writings are repeatedly quoted, fiercely contested, strongly asserted, and frequently misunderstood. For some people he has become a degraded symbol of a negative attitude toward sex and marriage, while for others he symbolizes purity from rampant sexual immorality in Western culture. Due to the sensitive nature of the controversy that surrounds this man, and the emotional intensity that often accompanies discussions of his statements, a study of his understanding of marriage and human sexuality is an important endeavor. Since in 1 Corinthians Paul has more to say on these topics than in any of his other letters, we will make it our text of study, attempting to understand the underlying reasons for the statements we read in this epistle.

The Apostle Paul was an extremely energetic man, and his ac-

complishments as a Christian missionary are truly remarkable. A seemingly tireless individual, he journeyed over an immense amount of territory during his missionary efforts to the Gentiles. Preaching the good news about Jesus Christ to those who had never heard the Gospel, establishing fledgling groups of new Christian converts, seeking to help believers grow in their faith, and correcting mistaken ideas in both belief and conduct, this industrious missionary exhibited a great amount of concern for the welfare of other people. His work met with stiff resistance from a number of individuals, however, and he was plagued with scores of problems from those who desired to thwart his missionary activities and subvert the message he proclaimed. Continually he found himself having to cope with the pressures imposed by those who rejected his claim to apostolic authority—stress resulting from repudiation of himself as a person and the belief system upon which his preaching was based. He was both loved and hated by many, and his letters reveal much about the ways in which Paul responded both to his friends and to his adversaries.

As a missionary pastor concerned for the welfare of the new Christian congregations he had established, Paul attempted to stay in touch with his converts when he left them and moved on to preach the Gospel to still others. Primarily he desired to be with them personally so that he could give aid in whatever manner might be needed. Yet there were times when personal visits were either not possible or not practical, and during these times Paul was forced to write letters and send them via trusted messengers. The letter carrier was usually one of Paul's co-workers, and he or she[1] functioned as more than a mere postman. Often letter carriers in antiquity communicated verbally to the recipients a good deal of information from the sender of the letter that had not been written down.[2] Since the letters themselves, then, were only part of the total communication delivered from Paul by his messengers, recognition of this fact complicates our efforts at understanding the epistles of Paul in the New Testament.

As we read Paul's letters, we are seeing only a small portion of what was a much larger conversation between this missionary and his addresses. The original recipients of the letter were, of course, part of

this larger dialogue; and as they read a letter from Paul, they under-stood the issues he was addressing. There was no need for Paul to explain such matters in his letter, for his readers knew them well. Unfortunately, this means that when we read the same letter, without the benefit of knowledge of the continuing conversation between Paul and his original readers and the problems they faced, we often find ourselves wondering what Paul is talking about. Details that Paul assumed his readers knew—details that are extremely important for understanding the letter—are no longer accessible. Consequently, we are forced to perform some careful detective work when we read a Pauline letter, in an attempt to reconstruct partially the situation the apostle sought to address.

The difficulty of this endeavor may be illustrated simply with the following exercise. Borrow a personal letter from a person you do not know very well, a letter written to that person by another party whom you do not know at all. Analyze the letter thoroughly, and when you have finished your analysis, go to the person from whom you borrowed the letter and explain what you have concluded. Then find out how accurate you have been in your reconstruction of the circumstances surrounding the writing of the letter, as well as how precisely you have understood what the author of the letter meant when saying various things. Such an experiment will often be rather humorous, for we tend to misinterpret what someone has written when we were not part of the actual circumstances ourselves. If this is true for letters written by our own contemporaries, composed in our own language using forms of expression that are part of our own culture, you may well imagine the added difficulties imposed when reading a letter written in a different language and culture some two thousand years ago.

1 Corinthians is a great example of the frustrations involved in reconstructing the life-setting of a Pauline letter, the conditions that occasioned the letter's composition. On the one hand, it is clear that the church at Corinth was filled with major problems and that Paul was extremely frustrated in trying to correct these situations. On the other

hand, because Paul addresses so many different problems and problem makers, it is difficult to decipher the identity of the various people whom Paul seeks to correct and to figure out what it was that these splinter groups believed. Since the Corinthian church was so fragmented with antagonistic factions, and Paul had to address the whole church in the same letter, we must be very careful, both when seeking to understand the nature of the problems he sought to correct and when attempting to decide what Paul himself proposed as the appropriate alternative beliefs and practices.

From 1 Corinthians we learn that Paul wrote on the basis of three sources of information. First, there was a group of people who came from Corinth to Ephesus, where Paul was then residing (see 1 Cor. 16:8), representing the house of Chloe (1:10–12). They were either members of the family of Chloe or part of a house-church[3] that met in Chloe's home, and the message they bore to Paul was grim: The church at Corinth was split into rival factions, each confessing allegiance to a different Christian leader. Some were loyal to Paul, but others rejected his apostolic office and openly criticized him (for example, 4:18–21; 9:1–3). Paul's second source of information came from the verbal report of three of his supporters, specifically those who brought him an official letter from the Corinthian church (16:17). These men, Stephanas, Fortunatus, and Achaicus, were received warmly by Paul (16:17–18), since they represented to him a force for order in the chaos at Corinth. With them they had the third source of information for Paul, a letter drafted by the church in which a number of questions were posed to the apostle. We may see evidence for this in various places in 1 Corinthians, where Paul mentions the questions asked in the Corinthian letter (for example, 7:1, 25; 8:1). So many different things were being taught by various people in the church that his teaching was needed in order to answer the multitude of questions that had arisen. A number of these questions centered on issues of sexual morality, and consequently the letter of 1 Corinthians offers a large amount of information pertinent to our topic of study.

The Corinthian church posed a real challenge for the Apostle Paul. Simultaneously he had to try to correct erring parties whose beliefs were opposite from each other. Some in the church advocated complete sexual license, claiming that one should be unconcerned about norms of sexual conduct. To counteract this belief, we might expect Paul to stress rigorous abstinence as a means of counterbalancing the extreme sexual laxity. But if he stressed abstinence, he would play into the hands of others at Corinth who claimed that one should avoid all sexual intercourse, even with one's own mate. Forced to speak to both extremes in the same letter, Paul addresses first one and then the other, seeking to bring both to a healthy understanding of how God would want them to behave. Consequently, if we are to understand Paul correctly, we must distinguish which faction he is addressing in each passage we will be discussing, for his directives are designed to correct specific mistaken beliefs and practices. Without making such distinctions, we would be guilty of misunderstanding the Apostle.

We must remember that Paul wrote to men and women who lived in a cultural setting vastly different from the Jewish setting in which Jesus lived and preached. The majority of the Jewish people in Palestine believed that God would conduct a great final judgment, in which the eternal fate of every person would be determined, and that just prior to this last judgment God would raise each person bodily from the dead. The average Jew, therefore, had the expectation of experiencing a bodily resurrection and rejected the Greek viewpoint that only a person's soul would continue to exist in heaven.[4] In the Greco-Roman culture at Corinth, such a belief would have been ridiculed.

Under the influence of a rich heritage of Greek philosophical thinking, the Gentile inhabitants of Corinth would have been raised and educated with the belief that the physical body is rather like the tomb of the soul. From this viewpoint the soul comes from a higher realm and is temporarily forced to descend to the lower realm of the

physical, being imprisoned in a body. At death the soul is released from the body; and if the person lived virtuously during his or her lifetime, the soul ascends back to the higher realms.[5] Consequently, belief in a bodily resurrection would involve a seemingly absurd notion of the eternal soul not being liberated from the corruptible body, but the lowly body actually being raised into the nonphysical higher realms.

When Paul came to Corinth, proclaiming the resurrection of the dead as part of the Gospel, his message sounded foolishly, anti-intellectual to many. This held true even for some members of the church. Although they had initially accepted the Gospel and placed their faith in Jesus, they came to interpret the nature of Christian faith in a manner vastly different from Paul's teaching. Maintaining that there was no resurrection from the dead (15:12), they held a very low view of the body and anything else related to the physical realm. Their focus was supposedly directed toward the heavenly realms; and, in their opinion, through a spiritual experience with Christ they had actually already attained a sort of spiritual resurrection that lifted them above the rest of humanity.[6] Viewing themselves as a spiritual elite, or *pneumatikoi* (the Greek word for "spirit" is *pneuma*), they looked with disdain upon those whom they considered mere fleshly people (*sarkikoi*; the Greek for "flesh" is *sarx*). As evidence for their higher status, they placed a great emphasis on supernatural manifestations, particularly that of speaking in tongues. Unconcerned with the feelings of others during the times when Christians gathered for worship, the so-called *pneumatikoi* were extremely unruly in their use of speaking in tongues, disrupting the meetings and creating chaos. Consequently Paul found himself needing to discipline such people.

Paul did not share the opinion the *pneumatikoi* had of themselves, and in various parts of his letter he is very sarcastic toward these people. For example, following an extended effort at speaking against their concern with human wisdom in 1:18–2:16, he pointedly remarks in 3:1–3,

> And I, brothers, was not able to speak to you as spiritual people (*pneumatikoi*) but as fleshly (*sarkinoi*), as babies in Christ. I gave you

milk to drink, not food, for you were not yet able to eat. Indeed, you are still not able, for you are still fleshly people *(sarkikoi)*! For where there is jealousy and contention among you, are you not fleshly people *(sarkikoi)* who live according to merely human ways?

Paul asserts that these people who fancy themselves elite are in reality fleshly babies in Christ. They are not really *pneumatikoi*; they are self-centered egotists who justify their carnal behavior by making lofty spiritual claims. In fact, there is another term that more suitably describes them—libertines.

Morally speaking, the libertines indulged in anything they desired. For example, they saw nothing wrong with continuing their pre-Christian practice of attending feasts held in honor of various deities in the temples of Corinth, even if this involved sexual rites (8:1–13; 10:20–22). In their opinion it was acceptable to visit prostitutes (6:15–18), since they believed that the body was so unimportant that what they did with it was inconsequential. They held a perverted notion of freedom in Christ—freedom to do whatever suited them, for Christ had liberated them from life in the physical realm. We may find a capsulized statement of their belief in 6:12–13: "All things are proper for me. Food is for the stomach and the stomach is for food, and God will destroy both." We might paraphrase this creed as follows: "All my desires are meant to be gratified. If I am hungry, I should eat; and if I am sexually stimulated, I should gratify my desire. Both my body and food are merely physical objects anyway, and they will perish."

Quite in contrast with the viewpoint of the libertines, there existed another group in the church at Corinth who were opposed to all sexual pleasure. Apparently, these people also held a low view of the body, only they espoused a position the extreme opposite of that of the libertines. They practiced asceticism, a renouncing of the pleasures of the body in effort to liberate the eternal part within them, the soul, from bondage to the physical body. As a result they probably envisioned some sort of spiritual union with Christ that their rigorous treatment of their bodies would make possible. Thus, denial of pleasure would release them from focusing on bodily concerns and make them super-spiritual. We will call these people the ascetics.

The ascetics were trying to convince married couples that they should abstain from sexual intercourse with their mates and live lives of total abstinence. Their slogan is expressed in 7:1: "It is good for a man not to touch a woman." When we compare this denial of the body with the wholehearted approval of sexual pleasure within marriage in the Old Testament, especially in the Song of Songs, we could hardly imagine a greater contrast. The Hebrews affirmed the belief that creation was good because God had made it; and when one lived according to God's order, a pleasurable life could be accepted gratefully as a gift from the Creator. The Greeks, however, often made a sharp separation between God and the physical world, and the effect of such thinking led to the libertine and ascetic tendencies in the church at Corinth. Paul deals with both extremes by emphasizing the importance of the physical body in the spiritual dimensions of living in obedience to God.

Expulsion of an Incestuous Man from the Church

So arrogant were the libertines over their freedom in Christ that they were proud of a situation in the church which was outlandish enough to shock even the city of Corinth. A member of the church was living with his father's wife, presumably his stepmother (5:1).[7] Paul does not say whether or not the man's father was still alive, so we do not know whether the woman involved was a widow or whether she and her husband were divorced. The Apostle calls the behavior *porneia*, a catch-all term for Paul that denotes fornication: any sort of illegitimate sexual activity,[8] including such things as prostitution and premarital sex. Since the Greek word for adultery is *moicheia*, it is possible that Paul would have used this term if the fornicator's father were still alive and/or still married to the woman involved. The indication given by 5:1 is not that the man and his stepmother were involved in an affair on the sly but that they were openly living together. Such a relationship was shocking even to the Greco-Roman world, whose sexual standards were considerably lower than those of Paul.

In antiquity, it was widely believed that there was something particularly abhorrent about a man having sexual relations with a woman who had belonged to his father. From a Jewish perspective, Leviticus 18:18 and Deuteronomy 22:30 and 27:10 strictly forbid it, and Mishnah, *Sanhedrin* 7:4 specifies,

> These are they that are to be stoned: he that has connection with his mother, his father's wife, his daughter-in-law, a male, . . . with a girl who is betrothed, . . . He that has connection with his father's wife is thereby culpable both by virtue of the law of the father's wife [that is, Lev. 18:8] and of another man's wife [that is, Lev. 18:20], whether in his father's lifetime or after his father's death, whether after betrothal [only] or after wedlock.[9]

Marriage to a wife of one's father was forbidden by Roman law also, even if the father were dead.[10] The famous statesman Cicero, denouncing a seemingly less perverse union between a mother-in-law and her son-in-law, expresses his dismay by saying, "Oh! to think of the woman's sin, unbelievable, unheard of in all experience save for this single instance! To think of her wicked passion, unbridled, untamed!"[11] Yet in spite of the well-recognized nature of cultural aversion to his action, a church member at Corinth exempted himself from the rules of society and openly lived with his stepmother. Such outlandish behavior was a matter of boasting on the part of the libertines, seemingly because it served as a great example of their freedom in Christ. Paul did not share their pride in their liberated ethics.

From Paul's perspective the guilty man's behavior was so heinous that he was to be removed from the Christian fellowship. We can detect a deep sense of dismay as the Apostle writes,

> It is actually reported that there is fornication among you, and such a fornication which does not even occur among the Gentiles; for a man is living with the wife of his father. And you are proud of it! Should you not rather have grieved so that you would have removed the one who did this from your midst?

He goes on to prescribe a solemn meeting of the church in which the fornicator is formally banned from their fellowship and thus from the fellowship of all Christians. Excluded from the people of God, namely, those who have entered into a new covenant with God through Jesus Christ, the offender is to be placed back into the ungodly realm of humanity where Satan holds sway over people. Paul evidently thought that the man would die when removed from the protective community of Christians under the rule of Christ, for he says ominously, "Deliver this one to Satan for the destruction of the flesh in order that his spirit might be saved on the day of the Lord" (5:5).[12] The very puzzling nature of this pronouncement once again illustrates the frustrations involved in interpreting Paul's letters. If only we knew what Paul's original readers understood about this matter, so much could be clarified!

In opposition to the libertines, Paul asserts in 5:6–8 that Christians should maintain a standard of sexual purity consistent with their new identity in Jesus Christ. All Christians, not just a few rigorists, should keep this level of purity. Comparing the church to a batch of bread dough, he employs the metaphor of yeast, a symbol for evil both in the Jewish[13] and in the Greco-Roman world,[14] and states that all yeast must be removed from the church. Paul compares the corrupting influence of the man who was living with his stepmother to the fermenting action whereby a small amount of yeast can spread and cause fermentation to occur in a whole batch of dough.

Paul's own philosophy toward Christian ethics is beautifully summed up in 5:7a: "Cleanse out the old leaven in order that you might be a new lump of dough, as you are—unleavened." In other words, "Be what you already are!" At the time of their conversion, these people were made pure in Jesus Christ. Now they must live lives that are consistent with the purity that is theirs by virtue of being incorporated into the body of Christ. Paul will return to this concept in 1 Cor. 6 to explain its meaning further.

Immediately after his command concerning the purification of the church, Paul decides to clarify a misunderstanding that had arisen as a result of a letter he had written to them prior to 1 Corinthians. In

this letter, which is no longer extant,[15] he had told them not to associate with fornicators *(pornoi)*, and they were confused over whether he meant Christian or non-Christian fornicators. Paul's response is very clear:

> I wrote to you in the letter not to associate with fornicators. This certainly does not mean with the fornicators of this world or with the covetous and swindlers, or idolaters, for in order to do that you would have to leave the world! I wrote to you not to associate with anyone who is called a brother [that is, a Christian] who is a fornicator or covetous person or idolater or abusive person or a drunkard or a swindler. Do not even eat with such people! For what business is it of mine to judge those outside [the church]? Should not you judge those inside? God judges those who are outside. Drive out the evil person from your midst!
>
> *(5:9–13)*

Christians have no control over the immoral behavior of those outside their fellowship, but they are responsible for maintaining high standards for themselves. Allowing unrepentant immoral people, who claim to be Christians, to continue to enjoy table fellowship in the congregation only allows their evil influence to affect others adversely. Paul expects immoral behavior from those in Corinth who are not Christians; but, as we will see in 1 Cor. 6, such behavior patterns are supposed to terminate when people make their allegiance to Jesus Christ.

Christian Sexual Ethics Versus Greek Cultural Norms

Some members of the Corinthian church were defrauding others in the church and were even taking them to court in their efforts at extortion (6:1–8). Consequently, there must have been terrible tension among the Christians when they gathered for worship! With rival factions and embittered participants in civil cases in the city court, we may easily imagine why they were sending delegations to the Apostle Paul, seeking help to solve their many problems. We may also understand why

Paul was very exasperated with them. Presumably because the libertines were the main instigators of the law-court battles, since in their arrogance they appear to have cared little for the feelings of others, Paul makes a very sarcastic comment against those who consider themselves to be so wise and superior to others: "I say this to your shame. Does there not exist among you even one wise person who is able to judge in the midst of his brothers?" (6:5). He goes on to say that the fact that such disputes even exist is humiliating enough, without their taking their grievances before non-Christian law courts and defaming the church before the whole city.

In the context of speaking against this unscrupulous behavior, Paul explains that the proper mind-set for a Christian is exactly the opposite of the self-seeking attitude of the libertines. Clearly echoing Jesus' law of love, he says that they should rather be wronged than to do wrong to another (6:7). Then, in words intended to demolish the self-confidence of the libertines, Paul asserts that what a person does in this physical body is far from unimportant—it has eternal consequences:

> Do you not know that the unrighteous will not inherit the kingdom of God? Do not be deceived! Neither fornicators *(pornoi)*, nor idolaters, nor adulterers *(moichoi)*, nor men and boys who allow others to use them for homosexual acts *(malkoi)*,[16] nor male homosexuals *(arsenokoitai)*, nor thieves, nor covetous people, nor drunkards, nor abusive people, nor swindlers will inherit the kingdom of God. And these things some of you were, but you were washed, but you were made holy, but you were made righteous in the name of the Lord Jesus Christ and in the Spirit of our God.
>
> *(6:9–11)*

What the libertines consider to be of no consequence, Paul associates with a pre-Christian, sinful life-style—a way of life totally removed from the will of God. Those who misuse their own bodies and the bodies of others through fornication, adultery, or homosexuality are like people who abuse and rob others because of their own selfish desires. Instead of living a radical life-style of selfless love for other

people as Jesus taught, they see others as means to gratify their own craving.

Paul makes it perfectly clear that a radical new orientation to life occurs when a person becomes a Christian. Whereas before conversion a man or woman might have participated in fornication, adultery, or homosexuality, these activities should afterward cease, since they are part of an unholy, unrighteous life lived in separation from God. Sexual deviations such as these are part of the sinful existence that is common in the realm of Satan's rule over people (cf. 5:5); they have no place in the lives of those who would be part of the kingdom of love over which God himself rules. When a person places faith in Christ, he or she is purified and given a new life, a life-style of loving obedience to God and loving concern for other people. Loose sexual behavior is totally unacceptable for Christians, for it is a total denial of what God has done in their lives. Contrary to the beliefs of the libertines, true spirituality will be reflected practically in standards of ethical purity far above those of the surrounding culture.

For example, a very common practice in Greece was for wealthy men to have mistresses and/or other hired female companions. For a variety of reasons, this custom was generally accepted by the culture. Greek girls were typically betrothed around the age of fourteen to men who were between thirty and thirty-five years of age. Middle- and upper-class men sought to marry women who would produce the best children; they did not marry for companionship. The Greek women were typically secluded in the home, neither accompanying their husbands to social occasions nor even being visibly present when their husbands received guests into their own homes. Largely uneducated, and probably rather boring to be with due to their confinement, the Greek wives of upper- and middle-class men were not considered to be proper companions for social functions. The wives of poorer-class men were able to work with their husbands to a much greater degree than those of the rich and enjoyed more freedom to be in locations such as the marketplace. Dio Chrysostom, an ancient Greek author who was himself a wealthy man, wrote that there was much more companionship and affection between husband and wife among the poor than

there was among the rich.[17] For the rich, another class of women filled the need for companionship and pleasure.

In 451 B.C. a law was passed in Athens that "made a sharp distinction between natives and foreigners and denied civil rights to the children of mixed marriages."[18] As a result of this action, many foreign women were forced to become independent, with some resorting to selling sexual favors. Thus, there came to be a new class of professional prostitutes in Greek society. Over the years many of these women became wealthy; and although they were not citizens of the state, they were often highly respected. Many were glamorous, well educated, and witty, and therefore were delightful companions for the Greek men who had enough money to secure their favors. Unlike the secluded Greek wives, these women knew how to exhibit the charm and graces that made them desirable to accompany men to parties, and so on, not to mention their amorous abilities to titillate male sexual fancies. A valuable part of Greek society, these professional women were called companions or friends *(hetairai)*. We may clearly view their accepted role in the following quotation recorded by Athenaeus in a section of his book *Deipnosophistae* in which he praises the virtues of *hetairai*:

> We keep mistresses *(hetairai)* for pleasure, concubines for daily concubinage, but wives we have in order to produce children legitimately and to have a trustworthy guardian of our domestic property.[19]

Among the Christians at Corinth there were few men who were wealthy enough to have had access to *hetairai*, for Paul says in 1 Cor. 1:26 that the majority were from the lower strata of society: "Consider your station in life, brothers. Not many of you are wise by human standards, not many of you are powerful, and not many are well-born." This fact did not mean, however, that they did not have ample opportunity for sexual adventure. There were plenty of lower-class prostitutes who were easily within the price range of common men. In the literature of antiquity there are many references to prostitutes and brothels, especially in wide-open harbor towns like Corinth. The shoe of one of these streetwalkers was accidently preserved from the ravages of time; and,

when discovered, the shoe was found to have a wooden plate nailed to the sole. On this plate was written in Greek, "Follow Me." Thus, as the woman walked along the dusty streets of the city, her little sign would leave an impression in the dirt, a clear message to passersby of the nature of her vocation. Any interested man needed merely to "follow."[20]

In Greek culture, sex was simply a very normal aspect of life. Husbands were allowed to have extramarital intercourse, and this was not considered to be a violation of marriage. Also, as we will see in detail in Chapter 7, homosexual relations between men were quite common. There was, nevertheless, a distinct double standard in sexual matters, since the Greek wives were forbidden to have extramarital intercourse. The sexual liberties denied the women were considered to be perfectly legitimate for the men, with society as a whole frowning only upon excess.[21] And in the city of Corinth a man could certainly find excess!

Aside from the regular prostitutes, there were also women in the temples at Corinth who functioned as temple prostitutes. In Corinth, during the time Paul wrote his letters, men could participate in sexual rites with these religious prostitutes in honor of some deity (for example, Aphrodite). How prevalent this practice was during Paul's time is somewhat conjectural, but two centuries previously Corinth was widely known for its sexual worship. Strabo, a Greek geographer writing toward the end of the first century B.C., made the following comments about the condition of the old city prior to its destruction by the Romans in 146 B.C.:

> And the temple of Aphrodite was so rich that it owned more than a thousand temple-slaves, courtesans, whom both men and women had dedicated to the goddess. And therefore it was also on account of these women that the city was crowded with people and grew rich; for instance, the ship captains freely squandered their money, and hence the proverb, "Not for every man is the voyage to Corinth".[22]

The ancient city of Corinth had such a long-standing reputation for vice that the Athenian dramatist Aristophanes (c. 448–380 B.C.) appar-

ently coined the expression "to corinthianize" as a term for describing profligate living.[23] We must keep in mind, however, that the Corinth of Paul's day was different than the old city, which the Roman consul Lucius Mummius completely devastated in 146 B.C.

For more than one hundred years the site lay in ruins, until Julius Caesar refounded the city in 44 B.C. as a Roman colony. Initially the new city was populated with a variety of colonists, such as discharged Roman soldiers and freedmen from Italy. Soon thereafter Greeks also began to settle in Corinth, and we know from the discovery of an old synagogue inscription that there was also a Jewish population there. Due to the city's favorable location on a major trade route, this harbor town rapidly expanded in size and prosperity; and by A.D. 54, when Paul wrote 1 Corinthians, Corinth was very cosmopolitan in its population. There would therefore have been considerable mixing of the various cultures and a mingling of different views on sex and marriage.

Unlike the secluded Greek wives mentioned earlier, Roman women enjoyed many more rights and freedoms. In prior centuries there had been an extreme double standard, with only the wife being obligated to maintain marital fidelity. By the first century A.D., however, there had occurred a great weakening of the double standard, which was accompanied by a general decline in sexual morals among the Roman people. The descriptions in Horace's *Odes* and Petronius' *Satyricon* of the grossly decadent behavior among women are probably extreme, but they are not without some justification. Roman women could divorce their husbands; and, partly because many of the women attained economic independence, many marriages were only temporary unions.[24]

Moral decadence in the city of Rome became as proverbial as the reputation earned by ancient Corinth. Politically conscious men often married a series of women merely to advance their political careers, and tales of sexual perversion among the members of royal families abound in ancient literature.[25] Throughout the Roman empire moral decadence was common, and the harbor town of Corinth was no exception. The famous satirist Juvenal (c. A.D. 55–140) lampoons female perversity in his "Sixth Satire," providing us with crude caricatures of lustful

women as he supposedly writes to challenge a friend's plans to marry.
He begins by saying comically that chastity used to dwell on earth in
past ages but, along with justice, has retreated from the world, with-
drawing to heaven:

> To bounce your neighbor's bed, my friend, to outrage
> Matrimonial sanctity is now an ancient and long-
> Established tradition. All other crimes came later,
> With the Age of Iron; but our first adulterers
> Appeared in the Silver Era. And here you are in *this*
> Day and age, man, getting yourself engaged,
> . . . . Postumus, are you *really*
> Taking a wife? You used to be sane enough—what
> Fury's got into you, what snake has stung you up?
> Why endure such bitch-tyranny when rope's available
> By the fathom, when all those dizzying top-floor windows
> Are open for you, when there are bridges handy
> To jump from? Supposing none of these exits catches
> Your fancy, isn't it better to sleep with a pretty boy?
> . . . You were once the randiest
> Hot-rod-about-town, you hid in more bedroom cupboards
> Than a comedy juvenile lead. Can this be the man now
> Sticking his silly neck out for the matrimonial halter?
> And as for your insistence on a wife with old-fashioned
> Moral virtues—man, you need your blood-pressure checked,
>   you're
> Crazy, you're aiming over the moon.[26]

Juvenal goes on at length, describing the adulterous tendencies of
women, giving example after example filled with sarcastically lewd
descriptions. One of his crudest examples concerns the wanton behavior
of women in the temple of the love-goddess Venus, as he proclaims the
hopeless nature of having a marriage where either the husband or the
wife is faithful. Although his descriptions are exaggerated for the sake
of humor, they do witness to the grim reality of moral decadence in the
Roman empire.

In Corinth during Paul's time, uncertainty exists over the exact
magnitude of sexual worship of various deities in the local temples; but

we do know that, for the non-Jewish population, participation in such sexual activities carried no social stigma. Furthermore, there are indications that the libertines actively participated in festivities in the temples, either in honor of Aphrodite or other deities whose worship involved sacred prostitution. From 8:1–11 and 10:14–22 we know that some in the Corinthian church continued to celebrate in various temples, partaking in the meals held in honor of the various deities. Considering the fact that the libertines were proud of the man living with his stepmother (5:2, 6), it is not at all difficult to imagine that they did not scorn indulgence with temple prostitutes. Perhaps this practice is what Paul speaks against in the next section of his letter, 6:12–20.

Union with Prostitutes and Union with Christ

Occasionally in 1 Corinthians, Paul cites a slogan of a particular group in the church and proceeds to explain why it is wrong. Of course, the original readers of the letter would readily have understood what Paul was doing, but many readers today are merely confused by his approach. For example, in 8:1 Paul first indicates that he is going to answer the question posed to him in the official letter from the church: "Now, concerning food offered to idols." Then he cites the condescending slogan used by the libertines in reference to their knowledge that there is but one God, with which they justify their participation in the festivities held in pagan temples: "We know that we all have knowledge." Paul goes on to explain that such "knowledge" makes people arrogant and unconcerned about the needs of other people. He is sharply critical of those who are basing their behavior on their "knowledge" and who, in so doing, are greatly damaging the faith of other Christians. Applying the law of love that Jesus taught, Paul tells these Christians that they should be so concerned for the welfare of other people that they would choose to abstain even from legitimate pleasures if by doing so they would avoid causing another Christian's faith to be

damaged (8:7–13). Love, not personal desire, should motivate their actions.

As in 8:1–13, Paul begins section 6:12–20 by citing a libertine slogan and then debunking that motto in the sentences that follow. Their slogan is "All things are proper for me," and Paul retorts, "But not all things benefit me!" (6:12a). In 6:12b he repeats the slogan "All things are proper for me" and then states emphatically, "But I will not be under the power of anything!" The libertine rationale for their claim to absolute freedom follows in 6:13: "Food is for the stomach and the stomach is for food, and God will destroy both." That they used this saying as a way of justifying their own practices of satisfying their sexual appetites is clear from Paul's immediate reply: "But the body is not for fornication but for the Lord, and the Lord is for the body!" (6:13). Flatly rejecting their devaluation of the human body as merely something that will be destroyed just like food, Paul states that the body is of great importance.

According to Paul the body is the place in which service to God is now rendered, and in the future it will be resurrected by God to enjoy eternal life (6:14). Unlike the libertines, who viewed the body as a useless shell to be discarded at death, Paul believed that the body is actually united with Christ in some sort of spiritual union during this physical existence (6:15a, 17).[27] Consequently, the Christian's body is actually called the temple of the Holy Spirit, who dwells within all who have placed their faith in Christ (6:19). Therefore the believer's body is not to be part of any impure activity, for it is the dwelling place of the living God through the Holy Spirit. Paul concludes that the Christian's body is not his or her own possession any longer, because it now belongs to God: "You were purchased in honor, therefore glorify God with your body" (6:20).

Whereas the libertines saw no conflict between their faith in Christ and their visiting of prostitutes, Paul saw such behavior as a total contradiction of faith:

> Do you not know that your bodies are members of Christ? Shall I therefore take the members of Christ and make them members of a prostitute? Never! Or do you not know that the one who is united with

a prostitute is one body with her? For the Scripture says, "The two will be one flesh." But the one who is united to the Lord is one spirit. Flee fornication! Every other sin which a man commits is outside his body, but the one who fornicates sins against his own body.

(6:15–18)

The concluding comparison between fornication and other sins is perhaps an overstatement made for the sake of emphasis, but there can be no doubt that Paul had strong feelings concerning this matter. A man who visits a prostitute harms himself. Having been cleansed from sin through the sacrificial death of Christ so that he might glorify God in his body (6:11, 20), if he now commits fornication, he completely contradicts the work of God in his life. Furthermore, the Christian must consider the woman with whom he has united in sexual intercourse.

The libertines placed sexual relations on the same level as eating a meal—mere gratification of a physical urge. Paul will not tolerate this attitude. The human body is not an impersonal object but is part of the total person. Since the body is not a mere shell but embodies person-hood, it is to be respected and treated with honor. To engage in sexual intercourse with a prostitute is not merely an impersonal act but is the union of two persons. Sexual union cannot be devalued to the purely utilitarian basis of gratification of desire—like eating when hungry. A man may legitimately use food, but he cannot use a woman, for she is a person, not an object.

Since much of Paul's argument is based upon the contradiction of a member of Christ becoming a member of a prostitute, it is possible that in this passage he is speaking of visiting prostitutes in pagan temples. If so, then the meaning of his words would be interpreted somewhat differently. Paul would be saying that when a member of Christ (a Christian) joins himself with a temple prostitute, he is unit-ing himself with the worship of the deity whom the woman serves. Thus, he who has been dedicated to the service of God the Father through Jesus Christ would be placing himself in the service of a pagan deity. If this is Paul's intended meaning, then his use of Genesis 2:24 ("the two will be one flesh") is a symbolic use, and he would be

applying the one-flesh imagery to membership in the family of God, not to sexual intercourse per se.[28] In other words, when Paul speaks of the Christian's body as a temple of the Holy Spirit in 6:19, he would be contrasting it to the temple of an idol. Consequently, when he says in 6:18, "Flee fornication!" his command would almost be synonymous with his command in 10:14: "Flee idolatry!" As in 10:14–22, where he shows the incongruity of a Christian's participating in the feasts held in pagan temples to honor various deities and then also participating in the communion meal held in honor of Jesus Christ (cf. 11:23–26), Paul would be pointing out the absurdity of giving oneself to Jesus and then giving oneself to another deity through union with a temple prostitute. Although the libertines would object and say that because there really is no God other than the Father of Jesus Christ, and therefore going to the temples of idols means nothing (see 8:4–10), Paul insists that visiting a temple prostitute is an act of unfaithfulness to God, a participation with idol worship. Thus, in 10:20–21 he asserts, "What the Gentiles sacrifice, they sacrifice to demons and not to God, and I do not want you to become partners of demons. You cannot drink the cup of the Lord and the cup of demons! You cannot share the table of the Lord and the table of demons!"

Celibacy as an Ideal: Is Sex Contrary to Spirituality?

Whereas in 1 Cor. 6, Paul is responding to information he received from oral reports, probably from Chloe's people (1:11) and those who brought the official letter from the Corinthian church (16:17), in 7:1 he begins to answer the questions posed by their letter: "Now, concerning what you wrote." At this point 1 Corinthians assumes a question-and-answer format as the Apostle attempts to provide direction for his confused converts at Corinth. With this change in format also comes a change in the source of the problems. In chapters 5 and 6 Paul addresses problems caused by the perverted notions of the libertines, but in chapter 7 the questions have arisen due to the teaching of the

ascetics. Their tendency was to reject sex entirely, as may be seen from their motto, which Paul quotes in 7:1: "It is good for a man not to touch a woman." Evidently they were teaching people that if they really wanted to be spiritual, they should become celibate. Consequently the church's letter posed questions such as the following to Paul: Should married couples continue to engage in sexual intercourse? Should widows, widowers, and divorcees remarry? Should a Christian who is married to a non-Christian seek a divorce so as not to be defiled by union with a nonbeliever? Should engaged couples marry and consummate their relationships or simply remain engaged and stay virgins? Paul's answers to these questions reveal a great deal about his understanding of sex and marriage.

Paul first addresses the legitimacy of sexual intercourse within marriage. Fully aware of the ever-present temptations for fornication in Corinth, and painfully cognizant of the difficulties these Greek Christians had in giving up their old sexual habits, he wisely advises,

> Because of fornication let each man have his own wife and each woman her own husband. Let the husband give what is due to his wife [that is, sex] and likewise let the wife give what is due to her husband. The wife does not have authority over her own body, but the husband. Likewise the husband does not have authority over his body, but the wife. Do not deprive each other, except by mutual agreement for a time in order that you might have more leisure to pray; and then return to normal relations, so that Satan will not tempt you because of your lack of self-control.
>
> *(7:2–5)*

Paul does not agree that married people should abstain from normal sexual relations in order to be more spiritual. As a matter of fact, he says that regular intercourse is an excellent deterrent for fornication. In saying this, his advice is very similar to that of the Hebrew sage whose words we read in Prov. 5:15–23, who advised that delighting in one's own wife will help preserve a man from "the loose woman." Paul does not view sex as a questionable activity for married Christians. Indeed, he commands husbands and wives not to deprive each other unless both

agree that they would benefit from a time of abstinence. He does not think that it is right for either husband or wife to withhold sexual favors, denying the desire of the other. Amazingly egalitarian in this matter, he states that the married person's body belongs to his or her mate.

To say that the wife's body belonged to her husband would have been to reflect a common belief, but to say that the husband's body belonged to his wife would have been to make a statement that would have shocked and perhaps offended those who heard it.[29] There are a few parallels in Jewish literature to Paul's mention of abstaining in order to pray, but they are strictly from a male perspective. The Testament of Naphtali 8:8 reads, "For there is a season [*kairos*, "time," as in 1 Cor. 7:5] for a man to embrace his wife, and a season to abstain therefrom for his prayer."[30] Time limits are set on this practice, however, in the Mishnah. The conservative Pharisaic school of Shammai taught that a man could take a vow to have no sexual intercourse with his wife for up to two weeks. The school of Hillel, on the other hand, limited such vows to one week unless the husband wanted special time to devote to study of the Torah. In such cases a laborer was still only allowed one week, whereas a scholar of the Law could take a vow of abstinence without his wife's permission for thirty days.[31] This regulation in the Mishnah goes on to say that if a woman refuses sexual intercourse to her husband, he may diminish her dowry (which he must return to her if he divorces her) seven denars a week. Conversely, if he refuses his wife, he must increase her dowry three denars for every week. So, although provision was made for the wife, a man could simply inform his mate that he was suspending their intercourse for up to thirty days while he studied the Scriptures—whether she liked it or not. For Paul such an arrangement could only be made by mutual consent; it could not be imposed by one partner upon the other.

Although Paul allowed for short times of abstinence, it is unclear whether or not he believed that these times were as spiritually beneficial as did some at Corinth. After his directive on such matters in 7:5, he says in 7:6, "And I say this as a concession, not as a command." What is not clear is whether this verse is a concluding statement to

7:1–5 or an introductory statement to the next passage in his letter. On other occasions in 1 Corinthians Paul makes similar use of "this" to refer ahead to what he is getting ready to say (see especially 7:29; 11:17; cf. 1:12; 7:26), so we must decide from context whether 7:6 serves to conclude or to introduce. When the letter was originally written, there were no paragraph divisions in the text. For that matter, documents were written entirely in uppercase Greek letters and rarely had any spaces between words or sentences, and punctuation marks were seldom used. Lowercase letters were a later invention, and consistent use of a standard set of punctuation marks did not occur until many centuries later. So when we read nicely punctuated sentences set off in paragraphs in our Bibles today, we are relying upon the well-educated judgments of scholars who have worked carefully with the numerous extant copies of copies of Greek manuscripts.

Unfortunately, we have none of the original autographs of any of the biblical books. By carefully comparing the numerous Greek manuscripts with all of their usually minor differences from one another, we are able to determine with a fair degree of confidence approximately what Paul, for example, originally wrote. We must not be deceived into regarding this as an exact science, however, for we are forced to work with probabilities when seeking to reconstruct the original text. Such is also the case with delineating units of thought in biblical texts. Deciding whether 7:6 is a conclusion or an introduction is a difficult decision to make.

If 7:6 is a conclusion, it seems best to regard Paul as saying that, in allowing for brief times of abstinence, he is giving a concession to the ascetics.[32] In other words, he does not believe that sex is somehow unfit for a Christian, or that abstaining will make a person more spiritual; and he certainly is not commanding people to abstain. He is only making a concession instead of forbidding abstinence altogether. If, on the other hand, 7:6 is an introduction, then Paul is alerting his readers to the fact that what he is about to say is not a command when he says, "And I desire all men to be as I am myself, but each has his own gift from God: one's gift is celibacy while another's is marriage" (7:7). Some ancient Greek manuscripts lend support to this connection

between 7:6 and 7:7 in that they record 7:7 as beginning *"For* I desire . . ."* rather than *"And* I desire . . ."* Although this textual variant is not necessary to make the connection between verses 6 and 7, it does somewhat enhance the probability of doing so. If Paul meant to connect these two verses, then together they form an introductory comment to what he goes on to say in 7:8 about remaining single. In effect he would be saying, "Now what I am about to say is not a command; because I am fully aware that, even though I am so satisfied with my own unmarried condition that I could wish that all were like I am, God gifts people differently, some with marriage and some with celibacy."

Paul was content in his single state, so much so that he could without hesitation recommend it to others as a desirable way of life. This contentment was evidence or validation to him that celibacy was God's will for his life. He was not, as some have accused him of being, an uptight bachelor who was bitter toward and suspicious of women. Paul's attitude toward women and marriage was healthy. We find in 9:5 that not having a wife was one of the sacrifices he had chosen to make for the sake of being able to minister to others more effectively. He realized, however, that God had not given to all Christians the ability to be contentedly single, so he says, "And I say to the unmarried and to the widows, it is good if they remain as I am. But if they cannot exercise self-control, let them marry, for it is better to marry than to burn (with passion)" (7:8–9). We must not think that Paul was some-how sexless—that he had no desires. He does not at all say that the contentedly single person will have no desire, but that he or she will be able to exercise "self-control." In other words, their desires are man-ageable, not causing them to be frustrated all the time. For those whose desire is stronger, causing them, figuratively, to burn with sexual passion, they will be more content if they are married. Paul does not exalt celibacy as a state that all truly spiritual people should seek to attain, as did the ascetics. His own celibacy is God's desire for *his* life, whereas most of the other apostles have wives (9:5).

Within the New Testament the term *unmarried (agamos)* occurs only in 1 Cor. 7. Although in classical Greek literature *agamos* is used

to refer both to those who have never been married and to those who were once married but presently are not,[33] there are some reasons to suspect that Paul uses *agamos* in 7:8, 11, 32, and 34 as a technical term denoting only someone who was previously married. In 7:8 *agamos* designates a group that is associated with "widows" and quite possibly means widowers; and 7:11, speaking of a woman who is separated from her husband, says that she should either remain "unmarried" *(agamos)* or be reconciled to her husband. Finally, in 7:34 Paul speaks of two groups of single women, the "unmarried" and the "virgins." Thus, verses 8 and 34 distinguish the "unmarried" from "widows" and "virgins," and verse 11 specifically identifies the unmarried woman as one who is separated from her husband. It is therefore possible that *unmarried (agamos)* in 1 Cor. 7 designates a widow, widower, divorced, or separated person,[34] whereas the term *virgin* is used to describe those who have never been married. If this is in fact the case, then Paul is identifying himself with the unmarried, meaning that at some previous time he had been married. We should recognize that this is conjectural, however, for Paul nowhere specifically mentions ever having had a wife.

Divorce and Remarriage: What About the Unbelieving Mate?

Under the influence of the ascetics' teaching, some had already separated from their mates, so Paul gives the following directives:

> And to the married I command, not I but the Lord, a woman should not be separated from her husband—and if she is already separated, let her remain unmarried or be reconciled to her husband. And a husband should not divorce his wife.
>
> *(7:10–11)*

For the matter of divorce Paul appeals directly to Jesus' command, which we studied in the last chapter. This is one of the very few times that Paul quotes a command of Jesus, and we notice the great author-

ity given to it. Yet he does not merely quote Jesus; he uses the saying to apply not abstractly to divorce as a concept but to the reality of divorce in Corinth. Jesus' command makes only a statement about divorce; so Paul discerns the logical extension of the implications involved in the command and then adds that those who have already separated themselves from their mates should either stay unmarried or else be reconciled to their mates. Note that here Paul is speaking to people who have initiated the separation; they are not merely the victims who have been divorced. He will later speak to such people, but here it is to the initiators that he says, "Stay unmarried or be reconciled."

Others in the Corinthian church were married to people who had not become followers of Christ; and although they had not yet separated from their nonbelieving mates, under the prodding of the ascetics they were considering whether or not they should. Paul has no command of Jesus concerning marriage to nonbelievers, and he makes a distinction between his own words and those of his Lord: "And to the rest I say, not the Lord, . . ." (7:12). Nevertheless, he is their apostle, and he does expect them to obey what he says. And what he tells them is at odds with the ascetic viewpoint, for he affirms the permanence of marriage, even if one's mate is a nonbeliever. Showing great respect for the marriage bond, Paul says that the Christian should not initiate divorce if the nonbelieving husband or wife is content to remain married. Pointedly he asks in 7:16 concerning the possibility of conversion: "Wife, how do you know whether or not you might save your husband? Or husband, how do you know whether or not you might save your wife?"

The question some Corinthian Christians were puzzling over was, Does marriage to a nonbeliever defile the believer and the children? From the perspective of Paul's Jewish heritage, we might expect him to answer in the affirmative. Mishnah, *Yebamoth* 7:5, for example, specifies that if a Jewish woman's mother or father is of priestly descent and she marries a non-Jew, then her children by him are illegitimate. Furthermore, Mishnah, *Kethuboth* 4:3, makes it clear that Gentiles were considered to be unclean and their children born in unholiness. Only if they became proselytes could they conceive and bear children in holi-

ness. Nevertheless, we find that Paul does not view the Christian as defiled by a nonbelieving mate. Rather, he affirms that the reverse is true: The non-Christian mate and the children are made holy by the Christian parent. The Corinthian believers need not be concerned that God might disdain them or their children because of a nonbelieving spouse.

However, what if the non-Christian husband or wife is disgruntled with the believer, perhaps because of his or her new faith, and wants a divorce? In this case Paul's teaching is different: "But if the nonbeliever separates, allow him or her to separate. The brother or sister is not enslaved in such cases" (7:15). Although Christians should not initiate divorce, Paul states that when the nonbeliever initiates, the believer is free from that relationship, and the indication is that he or she is free to remarry.

Following his instructions to married and divorced people, Paul must next answer the question of whether or not virgins should marry or stay celibate. Before addressing this issue, however, he provides a set of general guidelines in 7:17–24 that outline a principle for life, with obvious implications for the way a person would make decisions concerning marriage. A capsule summary of his words would be: "Content yourself to remain in whatever state you found yourself at the time of your conversion. If you can better your condition, do so; but if not, do not worry about where you would rather be." People commonly associate happiness with some condition in which they do not live and mistakenly think that if only they could have this or be that, then they would be happy. According to Paul, contentment can be a present reality even in less than desirable circumstances. *Do not waste your life wishing, enjoy your life being!*

Engaged Couples: Should They Marry or Remain Virgins?

Some of the engaged couples in the church at Corinth were very puzzled as to whether it would be right for them to marry. Apparently the ascetics were telling them that they should remain betrothed and

never consummate their marriages. Interestingly, Paul partially agreed with the ascetics' advice, although he did not at all accept their reasons for giving such instructions. He found nothing wrong with marriage per se, but in light of present circumstances he did not think it advisable:

> Now concerning virgins I have no command of the Lord, but I give my opinion as one who has received mercy from the Lord to be faithful. I personally think that in light of the impending distress[35] it is good for a man to remain as he is. Are you bound to a wife? Do not seek to be free. Are you free from a wife? Do not seek a wife. But if you marry you do not sin. And if a virgin marries she does not sin. But those who marry will have affliction of the flesh, and I would spare you that. I tell you this, brothers, the time is getting close . . . . for the form of this world is passing away.
>
> *(7:25–29, 31).*

Paul stressed that it is no sin to get married. Marriage is, after all, a gift from God. Nevertheless, Paul thought that conditions were such that people would be better off if they remained single. Very simply stated, he believed that the end of the world had come, and very soon a time of great stress would come upon the world.

The early Christians inherited the belief from Jewish Apocalypticism that before the final consummation of time there would be a terribly severe period of turmoil for the entire world. Events connected with this end-time duress were termed the Woes of the Messiah, for the Jews expected the Messiah's advent to signal the last times. Since the Christians affirmed Jesus as Messiah, they thought that he would shortly bring history to a grand climax. When he wrote 1 Corinthians, Paul firmly believed that he would be living when Jesus Christ returned to earth to vindicate the righteous and to destroy the wicked. Expecting this to happen in the very near future, Paul was concerned for the welfare of his fellow Christians, who would experience extremely severe conditions as the world experienced its last great time of woe. Places in the New Testament such as the book of Revelation and Jesus' apocalyptic discourses in the Gospels (for example, Mark 13) give vivid descriptions of these coming cataclysmic events, and reading

these accounts allows us to appreciate why Paul cautioned against marriage. Understandably, he thought that it would be easier to cope with the coming hardships if a person did not have the added responsibility of a spouse and children.

Due to the serious nature of the rapidly approaching end-time troubles, Paul cautions against becoming too tied to worldly possessions and institutions that would soon pass away (7:29–31). Neither marriage, nor business, nor anything else in the world should become the focus of life. There is nothing inherently wrong with these, or with enjoying them, but if they become overly dominant, they will cause anxiety. Paul was well aware that a married person can be more concerned about worldly matters, due to anxiety over pleasing his or her mate, and consequently fail to focus on serving God (7:32–34). A single person, being without the responsibilities involved in maintaining a marriage relationship and all that it entails, is more free to devote his or her energies toward service of the Lord. So Paul's advice is motivated by tender concern for his Corinthian converts. This is very clear in the way he concludes his statement: "I say this to you for your own benefit, not in order to throw a noose around your necks, but to promote good order and devotion to the Lord without distraction" (7:35). In the words of Lionel Swain, "The greater the attachment to the things of this world (cf., vv. 33, 34) the keener the suffering when the final transformation takes place."[36]

In light of his beliefs concerning the imminent arrival of the end-time struggle between the forces of good and evil, Paul gives his final advice to engaged couples:

> If anyone thinks he is behaving indecently toward his virgin, or if his passions are strong and he feels that he must marry, let him do what he desires. It is no sin. Let them get married. But whoever has his desires firmly under control, not having a feeling of necessity, but he has control over his desire, and he has made his own decision in the matter, to keep his fiancée as a virgin, he will do well. Thus, the one who marries his virgin does well, and the one who does not marry will do even better.
>
> *(7:36–38)*

This passage seems to indicate that, due to uncertainty caused by what the ascetics were teaching, some engaged couples were delaying their marriages. Some were doing fine under these circumstances, untormented by the need to marry. Their sexual desires were under control and not causing major problems. Others, however, had very strong passions and a need to fulfill them, being extremely desirous of marriage. They very much fit the category that Paul mentioned in 7:9: "If they cannot exercise self-control, let them marry, for it is better to marry than to burn [with passion]." Those who were under no compulsion he advised to remain unmarried, but they should make such a decision of their own free choice, not because some ascetic told them to do so. Due to the rough times ahead, Paul thought that those couples who stayed single would do better than those who married, but he also believed that marriage was good and should not be criticized.

We should note that some translations of 7:36–38 translate this passage as if it were directed to a father who has kept his daughter unmarried for so long that he is beginning to feel guilty about his decision. Although linguistically possible, this translation has multiple problems and does not at all fit the context of 1 Cor. 7.[37] It is built on two considerations. First, the verb *gamizō* in 7:37 can be translated "to give in marriage," which would fit the role of the girl's father but not her fiancé. This view receives increased credibility when we observe that previously in 1 Cor. 7 Paul has used the verb *gameō* ("to marry") when speaking of couples getting married. However, the verb *gamizō* is extremely rare, and we should be very cautious about basing our interpretation of 7:36–38 upon an insistence that this verb be translated "to give in marriage." Numerous grammarians, lexicographers, and commentators have demonstrated that "to enter into marriage" is an acceptable translation of *gamizō*.[38] Secondly, the word *heupakmos* in 7:36 can mean "maturity"; and it is possible to translate verse 36 in reference to the young woman, namely that she is "past her bloom" (that is, getting older). Thus, because of her age her father feels that he wants to change his mind and give her in marriage. This translation, however, violates the flow of thought in the passage. Paul is speaking of the ability of engaged couples to decide whether or not to consum-

mate their marriages. He began to explain how they should reach their decision in 7:25–28, then digressed to talk about coping with the end-time stress, and so forth, in 7:29–35, and finally returned to the topic of engaged couples making their decisions on marriage in 7:36–38. Furthermore, it would sound very strange indeed if in 7:37 Paul is describing a father's consideration of his daughter's marital status when he says, "Whoever has his desires firmly under control, not having a feeling of necessity, but has control over his desire. . . ." Throughout the entire passage he is speaking to couples; he does not suddenly begin to address a father in verse 32.

Almost as an afterthought, Paul adds a word of instruction to widows in 7:39–40:

> A woman is bound to her husband for as long as he lives; but, if the husband dies, she is free to marry whom she desires, only in the Lord. But in my opinion she is more blessed if she remains single, and I think I also have the Spirit of God.

She is under no obligation to yield to ascetic teaching to remain single, even though Paul thinks it best if she stays single. Giving his advice as one who has faithfully understood the will of God, he disdains to lay down any law except how she should remarry if she so chooses. The widow should marry "only in the Lord," meaning either that she should only marry a Christian man or that she should reach her decision in full awareness of her obedience to God's leading. From Paul's viewpoint, however, to decide to marry out of full obedience to God would include a commitment only to marry a Christian man. This bit of advice then leads to his final comment about also having the Spirit, which is presumably a somewhat sarcastic parting shot aimed toward the dogmatic ascetics whose viewpoint he has rejected.

Conclusions

In 1 Corinthians we are able to see much about the Apostle Paul and his views on sex and marriage. The letter reveals that he was frustrated with the numerous problems in the church at Corinth and the arrogant

attitude on the part of some who rejected what he had taught. Sarcastic at times, he was nevertheless deeply concerned for the welfare of these people and genuinely desired to help them be obedient to God. Jesus' law of love was very influential on Paul, and we observe in various passages that he proposed this sacrificial love ethic as a rule for life that would solve their many problems (for example, 6:1–11; 13:1–13).

Sexually speaking, Paul rejected the extremes of both the libertines and the ascetics. Whereas the libertines believed that the body was unimportant and therefore they could fulfill all their sexual desires with no resulting effect on their spiritual lives, Paul maintained a high view of the body as the place in which service to God is rendered. Demanding that these Gentile Christians reject their former practices of visiting prostitutes, committing adultery, having homosexual affairs, and so on, he asserted that upon conversion a believer is purified by God and becomes a temple in which the Holy Spirit dwells. Therefore, Christians must maintain a standard of sexual purity far above that of the surrounding Greco-Roman culture, for they have been spiritually united with Christ into his mystical body, the Church.

On the other hand, Paul also rejected the ascetic view that truly spiritual people should abstain from all sexual intercourse. Endorsing the rightful place of sex within marriage, his teaching reveals that he held the same wholesome view toward sex and marriage that we have seen in the Old Testament and in Jesus' teaching. Paul's advice to single people, that it would be best for them if they did not marry, was based on his belief that the end of the world was about to occur and that a terrible time of stress was imminent. It was this belief, and his desire to help these Christians cope with the coming difficulties, that motivated him to caution against marriage.

Paul followed Jesus in the belief that celibacy was a viable option for Christians, and thus he rejected the rabbinic belief that it was a man's duty to bear children. His views of sexual morality *are* those espoused by the Jewish people, however, and he demanded that Gentile Christians abandon all extramarital sexual activity and adopt a strict moral code. Believing that he was living in the last days of the world's history, Paul sought to lead people into a redeemed relation-

ship to God through faith in Jesus Christ, a faith that would reveal itself in love for others and moral purity. This is a major theme in Paul's letter to the Romans, which we will now use as a basis for studying homosexuality in the ancient world.

Notes

1. A woman named Phoebe was quite possibly the one who carried Paul's letter to the church in Rome. She is highly commended for ministry to Paul and others in Romans 16:1–2.

2. William G. Doty, *Letters in Primitive Christianity* (Philadelphia: Fortress Press, 1973), p. 2.

3. The phenomenon of Christians meeting for worship in the home of one of the members was common in the early church. In 1 Cor. 16:19, for example, Paul sends greetings from the church that met in the home of Aquila and Prisca (cf. Romans 16:3–5; Colossians 4:15; Philemon 2).

4. For an explanation of the contrast between Jewish and Greek thought on this matter, see Oscar Cullmann, *Immortality of the Soul or Resurrection of the Dead?* (London: The Epworth Press, 1958).

5. The amount of ancient Greek material that deals with the soul and afterlife is vast. For example, in Plato's dialogues see *Phaedo* 106e–115a; *Phaedrus* 245c–57a; and *The Republic* X 608d–21d, especially the Myth of Er in 614b–21d.

6. Anthony C. Thiselton, "Realized Eschatology at Corinth," *New Testament Studies* 24 (1978): 510–26.

7. There is little possibility that the man was living openly with his biological mother. It is doubtful that even the libertines would have allowed such an absolutely forbidden action (read, e.g., *Oedipus Rex* by Sophocles). Hans Conzelmann, *1 Corinthians*, Hermeneia commentary series, trans. James W. Leitch (Philadelphia: Fortress Press, 1975), p. 96, lists references to ancient sources and says, "Such a marriage is inconceivable even in Greece and Rome." Yet see Tacitus, *Annals* 14, for an account of Emperor Nero's secret incestuous relations with his own mother.

8. The *porneia* word group occurs fourteen times in 1 Corinthians: *pornē* (prostitute) in 6:15, 16; *porneia* in 5:1 (twice); 6:13, 18; 7:2; *pornos* (male immoral person) in 5:9, 10, 11; 6:9; and the verb *porneuō* (to commit fornication) in 6:18; 10:8 (twice).

9. Trans. Herbert Danby, *The Mishnah* (Oxford, Eng.: Oxford University Press, 1933), pp. 391–92. Cf. Mishnah, *Kerithoth* 1:1 and *Yebamoth* 11:1. Note also that in Amos 2:7 God pronounces judgment because "a man and his father go in to the same maiden, so that my holy name is profaned." This is perhaps a reference to cultic prostitution, in which a father and son visit the same temple and therefore the same women. In 2 Samuel 16:20–23; 20:3, David's son Absalom did an extremely odious thing by forcing ten of his father's concubines to have sex with him. David would not touch these women after that time but kept them secluded and sexless.

10. Gaius, *Institutes* I.63.

11. *Pro Cluentio (In Defense of Aulus Cluentius)* 15. Trans. H. Grose Hodge, *Cicero: The Speeches*, The Loeb Classical Library (New York: G. P. Putnam's Sons, 1927), p. 237.

12. Timothy C. G. Thornton, "Satan—God's Agent for Punishing," *Expository Times* 83 (1972): 151–52, cites evidence that Jews sometimes identified Satan as God's agent for punishing evil people. For example, the "destroyer" in Exodus 12:23 is later called an angel of Satan in Jubilees 49:2. Similarly, God's plague of Numbers 16:41–50, which is said to have come from a fiery angel, is reported in 4 Maccabees 7:11, Wisdom 18:25, and 1 Corinthians 10:10 as a plague inflicted by Satan. Thornton also gives evidence from 1 Enoch and rabbinic literature.

13. Matthew 13:33; Luke 13:21; James 3:2–5; Philo, *On the Special Laws* I.193, *Questions and Answers in Exodus* 1:15.

14. E.g., Plutarch, *The Roman Questions* 289 (#109).

15. Many scholars believe that 2 Corinthians 6:14–7:1 is a fragment from this early letter.

16. Walter Bauer, *A Greek-English Lexicon of the New Testament and Other Early Christian Literature*, 4th ed., trans. rev. William F. Arndt and F. Wilbur Gingrich (Chicago: The University of Chicago Press, 1952), p. 489.

17. *Discourse* 7:65–80.

18. Friedrich Hauck and Siegfried Schulz, "πόρνη," in *Theological Dictionary of the New Testament*, vol. VI, ed. Gerhard Friedrich, trans. ed. Geoffrey W. Bromiley (Grand Rapids: Wm. B. Eerdmans Publishing Company, 1968), p. 582 (Plutarch, *Pericles* 37).

19. *Deipnosophistae* XIII. 573b. Trans. Charles Burton Gulick, *The Deipnosophists*, vol. VI, The Loeb Classical Library (Cambridge, Mass.: Harvard University Press, 1937), p. 95.

20. Hans Licht, *Sexual Life in Ancient Greece* (New York: Barnes & Noble, Inc., 1963), p. 338.

21. Hauck and Schulz, "πόρνη," p. 583.

22. *Geography* 8.6.20. Trans. Horace Leonard Jones, *The Geography of Strabo*, vol. IV, The Loeb Classical Library (New York: G. P. Putnam's Sons, 1927), p. 191.

23. Conzelmann, *1 Corinthians*, p. 12.

24. William H. Leslie, "The Concept of Women in the Pauline Corpus in Light of the Social and Religious Environment of the First Century" (unpublished Ph.D. dissertation, Northwestern University, 1976), pp. 416–17.

25. E.g., Tacitus, *Annals* 14, describes incest and murder by the Emperor Nero.

26. *Satire VI*, trans. Peter Green, *Juvenal: The Sixteen Satires*, the Penguin Classics (New York: Penguin Books, 1967), pp. 127–28. Reprinted by permission of Penguin Books Ltd.

27. Paul gives a full exposition of the resurrection in 1 Cor. 15.

28. For a defense of this interpretation, see G. R. Dunstan, "Hard Sayings—V," *Theology* 66 (1963): 491–93.

29. The Stoic philosopher Musonius was one of the very few who wrote a similarly egalitarian view on this matter. For a full quotation of the Greek text, see Johannes Weiss, *Der erste Korintherbrief* (Göttingen, Germany: Vandenhoeck & Ruprecht, 1910), p. 172, note 17.

30. Trans. R. H. Charles, ed., *The Apocrypha and Pseudepigrapha of the Old Testament in English*, vol. II (Oxford, Eng.: Clarendon Press, 1913), p. 339.

31. Mishnah, *Kethuboth* 5:6.

32. Some scholars believe that Paul is referring to all of 7:1–5, meaning that he views marriage itself as a concession due to the temptation to fornicate (e.g., Conzelmann, *1 Corinthians*, p. 118). This viewpoint ascribes to Paul the very ascetic tendency he is trying to combat.

33. E.g., Euripides, *Helen* 689, *Orestes* 205, *Suppliants* 786; Aeschylus, *The Suppliant Maidens* 143; Plato, *Phaedrus* 240A; Sophocles, *Antigone* 867; cf. 4 Maccabees 16:9.

34. William F. Orr, "Paul's Treatment of Marriage in 1 Corinthians 7," *Pittsburgh Perspective* 8, #3 (1967): 12–13, also affirms this view of *agamos*.

35. Greek *anankē* is typically translated "necessity" (e.g., 1 Cor. 7:37); but due to the clearly apocalyptic context indicated by 7:29–31, it is best translated "distress" in 7:26. Other apocalyptic uses of *anankē* occur in 4 Ezra 5:1–13; 6:18–24; 9:1–12; Jubilees 23:11–31; etc.; and the term is used of external distress in 2 Cor. 6:4; 12:10; 1 Thessalonians 3:7; Psalms of Solomon 5:8; and Testament of Joseph 2:4.

36. Lionel Swain, "The Bible and the People: Paul on Celibacy," *Clergy Review* 51 (1966): 789.

37. Jean Héring, *The First Epistle of Saint Paul to the Corinthians*, trans. A. W. Haethcote and P. J. Allcock (London: Epworth Press, 1962), pp. 63–64, details six reasons why it is extremely improbable that Paul is speaking of a father giving his daughter in marriage, and five reasons why he is surely addressing engaged couples.

38. E.g., James Hope Moulton and Wilbert Francis Howard, *A Grammar of New Testament Greek*, vol. II (Edinburgh: T & T Clark, 1929), p. 410; cf. vol. III, p. 57; F. Blass and A. Debrunner, *A Greek Grammar of the New Testament and Other Early Christian Literature*, trans., rev., ed. Robert W. Funk (Chicago: The University of Chicago Press, 1961), §101; Conzelmann, *1 Corinthians*, pp. 131, 36; C. K. Barrett, *The First Epistle to the Corinthians*, Harper's New Testament Commentaries (New York: Harper & Row, 1968), p. 185.

Romans 1:18-32: Homosexuality in Antiquity and Paul's Argument from Natural Order

Paul's Argument That
Homosexuality Is Contrary to Nature

Given the often violent controversies which surround the whole issue of homosexuality, it seems best to take special care to locate Paul's statements on this topic in the cultural setting of his day. Consequently, in this chapter we will look more extensively at the viewpoints on homosexuality represented by various segments of the first century culture in which Paul wrote. By so doing we will be able to understand more fully the true significance of the Apostle's words. In his time as well as in ours, there is great diversity of opinion as to the morality of homosexual relationships.

Perhaps the major New Testament passage on homosexuality is Romans 1:18–32, a text in which Paul labels this practice as a perversion of the natural order of creation. Employing homosexual relations as his ultimate example of Gentile perversity, the Apostle states with forceful clarity that those who perform such acts are under the wrath of God. Yet his primary purpose in this passage is not to attack homosexuals but to demonstrate that all men and women stand guilty before Almighty God, in need of forgiveness and grace. What he says about

homosexuality in Romans 1 is therefore different in orientation from material in 1 Corinthians on sexual matters. Whereas in 1 Cor. 5–7 Paul deals with specific problems in the Corinthian church that needed correction, in Rom. 1:18–32 it is doubtful that he is seeking to correct a particular problem in the church at Rome. The main thrust of the early chapters of Romans is not an attempt to teach ethical and moral behavior.

In Rom. 1–3 Paul speaks like a prosecuting attorney, presenting one piece of evidence after another, seeking to validate the claim he makes in 3:19, that everyone in the whole world stands guilty and condemned before God. Pointing his finger at the Jewish people, he says that they are guilty because, although they have the law of God in the Hebrew Scriptures, they have not kept the law (2:17–29). Paul cannot claim that the Gentiles are guilty on the basis that they have disobeyed God's law, however, since they do not have the Mosaic commandments. So the Apostle argues for Gentile guilt by appealing to nature. Asserting that they have willfully rejected the knowledge of God, knowledge that is readily available to them by merely observing the surrounding world, he states that their perverted morals and ethics are a direct result of their rejection of God. Thus, Paul's opinion of homosexuality is expressed within the larger argument, which he develops in Rom. 1–3, serving as his main example for illustrating that Gentiles are guilty and in need of God's grace. Unable to attain the righteousness needed for salvation, they are in need of redemption through Jesus Christ and the righteousness of God, which comes only as a gracious gift to those who place their faith in Christ (for example, 3:21–30).

Just prior to Rom. 1:18–32, Paul gives an important capsule statement that he goes on to elaborate in detail in the letter:

> I am not ashamed of the Gospel, for it is the power of God unto salvation for everyone who believes, to the Jew first and also to the Greek. For in it the righteousness of God is revealed from faith unto faith, as it is written: "The righteous will live by faith."
>
> *(1:16–17)*

Paul proclaims in his message that all people, Jews and Gentiles alike, obtain salvation through placing their faith in Jesus Christ. He stresses as forcefully as he is able that no one can earn salvation by his or her own effort. It is, of course, outside the scope of this study to trace how Paul argues that righteousness is given only as a gift of God to the man or woman of faith. What is important for us to notice at this time is that in order for Paul to establish that all people may receive God's gift through faith, he must first establish that all are equally in need of God's grace. So before he explains fully the good news of unmerited salvation, he details the bad news of the human evil and impotence that necessitates God's gift of righteousness.

First Paul brings charges against the Gentiles, launching a two-pronged attack on idolatry and immorality, which he links together in a cause-and-effect relationship. His purpose is not to explore all the different belief systems of Greeks, Romans, Persians, and so on, and explain how some are morally and ethically better or worse than others. Neither is it his desire to contrast the beliefs about deity espoused by various philosophical schools with those held by the general populace in locations throughout the known world, although he was certainly aware of such distinctions. Paul's purpose is to pronounce universal guilt, and he does so by lumping all Gentiles together and by making sweeping generalizations. His description is therefore intentionally very bleak, and his language is intended to impact the reader with the stark reality of Gentile sinfulness.

Paul charges in 1:18–20 that Gentiles have willfully and wickedly suppressed the truth about God. Claiming that all can see, merely by observing the world around them, that an eternal God of immense power created it all, he asserts that people are without excuse. Although God is invisible, he *has* revealed his existence to everyone through his creation, and there is no excuse for believing that the Creator is part of creation. Nevertheless, Gentiles have deliberately rejected this knowledge and have refused to glorify God and to thank him as Creator (1:21a). As a result, Paul says that their ability to reason became so diminished that they exchanged the glory of the eternal God for idols resembling perishable, created beings: humans, birds, four-

footed animals, and reptiles (1:21b–23). Far from being the wise individuals they fancy themselves to be, they are stupid fools, according to Paul, and their folly has placed them into a precarious situation.

The terrible exchange of God for idols, or the Real for the imagined, has brought about the frightful experience of the wrath of God. Although it was common for Jewish writers to believe that God was coming soon to execute judgment upon sinners, Paul's use of the present indicative tense of the verb in 1:18 to describe God's wrath is atypical. He states that God's wrath is a present reality: "For the wrath of God *is being revealed* from heaven against all ungodliness and wickedness of men who suppress the truth in wickedness." Generally this type of language about wrath was reserved for predictions of future events, such as the following prophecy from 1 Enoch 91:7:

> And when sin and unrighteousness and blasphemy
> And violence in all kinds of deeds increase,
> And apostasy and transgression and uncleanness increase,
> A great chastisement shall come from heaven upon all these,
> And the holy Lord will come forth with wrath and chastisement
> To execute judgment on earth.[1]

Paul also expected this great end-time judgment when God would lash out with awesome physical destruction of the wicked, vindicating the righteous by annihilating the sinners (Rom. 2:5, 8; 5:9).[2] Such an expectation was very much a part of the belief of the early church, as passages like Revelation 6:16–17; 19:15; Mark 13:19–31; and Matthew 24:15–35 reveal. Yet Paul's explanation of God's wrath in Rom. 1:18–32 is in terms not of future judgment but of present reality.

The terrible destruction brought about by this wrath is not at all like the end-time predictions of devastation by warfare, or like the consequences for breaking the covenant that we saw in Deuteronomy, or even like the social retribution described in Proverbs. In Rom. 1, Paul says that God in his wrath has allowed people to do what they wanted to do, permitting them to degrade themselves through their own perverse desires. Thus, the immoral practices of the Greco-Roman

world are seen as evidence that God has given people over to self-degradation, allowing them to become subhuman.

> Therefore God delivered them in the desires of their hearts over to uncleanness, the dishonoring of their bodies among themselves. They exchanged the truth about God for a lie and worshipped and served the creature rather than the Creator who is blessed forever. Amen. Because of this, God delivered them over to dishonorable passion, for their women exchanged their natural function for one that is against nature. Likewise the men also, abandoning the natural function of the woman, were inflamed in their desire for one another, men committing the shameless deed with men and receiving in themselves the penalty which their perversion deserves. And since they did not acknowledge God in their understanding, God delivered them over to a worthless mind, to do things which are not proper.
>
> *(Rom. 1:24–28)*

Paul believes that there is a clear connection between idolatry and immorality, as is revealed by his concept of the terrible *exchange*. The Gentiles exchanged the truth that was available to them about God for their own mythologies, choosing to worship and serve idols of created beings rather than the invisible Creator. When they thus chose the unreal for the Real, the result was a further exchange of the natural for the unnatural. Paul declares that simple observation of nature reveals the fact that God made male and female to find sexual fulfillment in the opposite sex. Merely noticing the construction of male and female genitalia makes this extremely obvious. Nevertheless, the Gentiles, who view themselves as wise, have become so stupid in their darkened logic that they have chosen the unnatural practice of homosexuality instead of the natural heterosexuality. Homosexuality is so degraded for Paul that he understands its very existence as proof that God must have abandoned those who practice it, allowing them to go against his natural created order because they refused to worship and serve him.

In the development of his argument in Rom. 1–3, Paul evidently chose homosexuality as his primary example of why the Gentiles are guilty before God, because he saw it as such an obvious violation of nature. Exchange of the natural sex roles for that which is unnatural is

closely tied with their prior exchange of God for idols. Since this exchange is in flagrant violation of natural law and represents a conscious choice to suppress truth, they can legitimately be judged by God. Their perversion is proof of their guilt.

Jewish Abborrence of Homosexuality

Paul's view of homosexuality is in harmony with the position expressed by many Jewish authors of antiquity. For the Jews, Gentile idolatry and Gentile sexual immorality were almost necessarily connected in a cause-and-effect relationship: If people worshipped idols, then of course they would be immoral! Adultery, incest, prostitution, and sexual worship of gods and goddesses were used as stock examples of Gentile perversion, but homosexuality occupied a special place of abhorrence for the Jewish people. The position of the Mosaic Law is abundantly clear: "You shall not lie with a man as with a woman: it is an abomination" (Leviticus 18:22). "If a man lies with a male as with a woman, both of them have committed an abomination; they shall be put to death, their blood is upon them" (Lev. 20:13). For Torah-loving Jews, homosexuality was a ridiculously sinful practice.

There is very little evidence that homosexuality was known among the Jewish people, although there are a few references to such actions in several passages contained in a collection of texts called "The Testaments of the Twelve Patriarchs." The Testament of Levi has statements of judgment leveled against wicked Jewish priests who are "idolaters, adulterers, . . . [and] abusers of children and beasts."[3] How much this is an accurate representation of the conduct of these men and how much this description is merely an attempt to defame them as enemies is rather uncertain. Elsewhere in the "Testaments" there are two passages that predict that in the last days some Jews will "depart from the Lord . . . and . . . do according to all the wickedness of Sodom,"[4] which refers back to the events of Genesis 19.

Gen. 19:1–28 recounts the story of two angels of God going to the city of Sodom to destroy it because of the terrible wickedness of the in-

habitants of the city. In appearance the angels looked like men; and while they stayed with a man named Lot, their true identity was not known. During the night the men of Sodom came to Lot's house and demanded that he give to them his two guests so that they could use them sexually. The account ends with Lot and his family fleeing to safety while God utterly destroyed Sodom and the nearby city of Gomorrah for their wickedness, raining down fire from the sky and totally annihilating the cities' inhabitants. This story became symbolic to many Jews of the way in which God would execute his wrath upon sinners in the future, during the last days. Furthermore, Sodom and Gomorrah became a symbol of wickedness and perversion, and "the sin of Sodom" was understood as homosexuality. Note, for example, the reference to Sodom in the following text, which was written before Paul's time and shows considerable similarity to his argument in Rom. 1:18–32:

> Sun and moon and stars change not their order; so do ye also change not the law of God in the disorderliness of your doings. The Gentiles went astray, and forsook the Lord, and changed their order, and obeyed stocks and stones, spirits of deceit. But ye shall not be so, my children, recognizing in the firmament, in the earth, and in the sea, and in all created things, the Lord who made all things, that you become not as Sodom, which changed the order of nature.[5]

We also find a strong aversion to idolatry and homosexuality in the Jewish Sibylline Oracles, documents written pseudonymously under the guise of the Roman Sibylline Oracles. Originally the Romans had a set of three books written by a sibyl, a woman who uttered rather obscure prophetic messages during trancelike states. These documents were believed to be supernaturally inspired, and during times of stress they were brought out of their special storage place and carefully studied for divine guidance. Gradually other texts were added to the collection, and a number of pseudo-Sibylline books were written by various interest groups, including the Jews. Partly as a means of denouncing Roman idolatry and immorality, Jewish authors wrote Sibylline Oracles, and some of their content reveals the same themes Paul presents in Romans 1.[6] Oracle III. 584–606, for example, while speaking of holy men who offer unblemished sacrifices to God, says,

For to them alone the Mighty God has given . . . an excellent understanding in their hearts: in that they give not themselves to vain deceits, nor honour the works of men's hands . . . likenesses of beasts. . . . Nor do they hold unholy intercourse with boys, as do the Phoenicians, Egyptians, and Latins, and *spacious* Hellas, and many nations of other men, Persians and Galatians and all Asia, transgressing the holy law of the immortal God which he ordained. For which cause the Eternal shall impose on all men retribution . . . and woes . . . pestilence and fearful calamities; because they would not honour in holiness the eternal Father of all men, but reverenced and honoured idols.[7]

While extremely similar to Paul's argument, this warning of coming retribution appeals to Mosaic law and not to nature for its condemnation of homosexuality, and it does not see homosexuality as evidence of God's present expression of wrath. Like other Jewish documents, the Oracle sees wrath as coming upon homosexuals for their perversion; it does not see wrath in the actual existence of homosexuality as a practice.

Slavonic Enoch, a Jewish document apparently written in final form in Alexandria during the first half of the first century A.D., says the following as part of a description of the tortures received by the wicked after their death:

This place, O Enoch, is prepared for those who dishonour God, who on earth practise sin against nature, which is child-corruption after the sodomitic fashion, magic-making, . . . [there follows a list of vices similar to Rom. 1:29–31] . . . who knew not their creator, and bowed down to soulless [sc. lifeless] Gods, who cannot see nor hear, vain gods, *who also* built hewn images. . . . (10:4–6)[8]

In this passage homosexuality is classified with other activities considered to be unnatural, such as stealing, murder, and fornication. Idolatry and vice are seen as parallel sins, however, and vice is not described as arising from idolatry.

The viewpoint presented by Paul in Rom. 1:18–32 finds its closest Jewish parallel in the first century B.C. document called the Wisdom of Solomon. Written in Alexandria, its teaching on the connection between idolatry and immorality is so close to Paul's that we

might reasonably claim that Wisdom, or other documents like it, were very instrumental in shaping Paul's thought, either directly or indirectly. Going into much more detail than does Paul, Wisdom 13:1–14:7 explains how foolish people studied the world but failed to recognize God as the Creator. Ignorantly they postulated that various parts of nature were in control of the world, or certain aspects of it, and they made lifeless idols of wood, stone, or metal and prayed to these instead of to the eternal God. Wisdom 14:8–12 proceeds to predict God's future judgment upon idolatry and makes the same connection as does Paul when it asserts: "For the idea of making idols was the beginning of fornication, and the invention of them was the corruption of life" (verse 12). This concept is further developed in Wisdom 14, where in verse 27 the specific claim is made: "For the worship of idols not to be named is the beginning and cause and end of every evil."

Paul was certainly not alone in his claim that Gentiles were without excuse for failing to recognize God as the eternal, invisible Creator; nor was he unique in saying that idolatry leads to immorality. However, there do not appear to be any extant ancient Jewish texts that state that the very existence of homosexuality is evidence that God in his wrath has allowed men and women to pervert themselves. This concept appears to be uniquely Pauline. The Jewish authors would agree wholeheartedly with Paul that homosexuality is perverse, but their explanations of its origin and practice varied. This is especially evident in the work of Philo.

A Jewish Philosopher's Denunciation of Homosexuality

Typically in ancient Jewish condemnations of immorality there was little or no attempt made at formulating a sustained explanation of why activities like homosexuality are evil. Philo of Alexandria (30 B.C.–A.D. 45), however, was a Jewish philosopher who gave considerable attention to such matters. He was very well educated in Greek philosophy, and his thought was largely molded by the teachings of Plato and others. Nevertheless, he was also a faithful Jew who held to his ances-

tral faith as the truth revealed by God. One of his major goals in writing was to demonstrate to Gentiles that the laws of Moses were in fact based upon the purest philosophy; and, when understood allegorically, they must be placed above all other written works. Practically speaking, this means that Philo generally explained Jewish customs and beliefs predominantly through argumentation based upon Greek philosophy. This is especially interesting when he explains why homosexuality is evil.

Unlike Paul, Philo attributes the origin of homosexuality not to idolatry but to excess wealth. In his work *On Abraham* 134–44, he explains that vice increased in Sodom because of the high productivity of the land. There was such a plentiful food supply that the city's inhabitants fell prey to "the chief beginning of evils . . . goods in excess."[9] Philo says that they were unable to cope successfully with such satiety and became beastlike, pushing and shoving each other like cattle in a feeding area. They "threw off from their necks the law of nature,"[10] the way humans are supposed to behave, and immersed themselves into a totally nonphilosophical life-style. Philo himself espoused a philosophical ideal of thoughtful contemplation of life and moderation in eating, drinking, and so on, so it is not surprising that his portrayal of Sodom's residents is one of irrational animals. He states that the men's mad lust not only caused them to have sexual intercourse with their neighbors' wives, but they also ignorantly "mounted males without respect for the sex nature."[11] Rather humorously Philo says that these men were so stupid that they were dismayed when they discovered that they could not bear children through their sexual relations with males. But even when they figured this out, they were too immersed in the practice to stop, for the force of their lust for men was so strong that it totally mastered any rationality that remained.

We also discover that Philo detested homosexuality because of his view that men were superior to women. Thus, when a man played the passive role characteristic of a woman in sexual relations, he debased what he was by nature and took on "the formidable curse of a female disease."[12] For Philo, women were inferior beings, and only the madness of irrational lust would cause a man to become effeminate. Fur-

thermore, if such homosexual passion became widespread, he asserts that the human race would become extinct. Therefore, Philo explains that God richly blessed the marriage unions of men and women by giving to them many children, but he invented a startling new method of punishing Sodom's depraved men. Since Sodom's residents engaged in "unnatural and forbidden intercourse,"[13] God had his two angels rain fire from heaven and reduce the city to smouldering ruins.

In the viewpoint of Philo, sexual intercourse is only natural when it leads to reproduction. Any sex that is based upon passion and not reproduction is perverse; and therefore homosexuality is the most perverse, since no reproduction can result from it. Consequently he attributes it to an abominable lust, which "forces the male type of nature to debase and convert itself into the feminine form, just to indulge a polluted and accursed passion."[14]

According to Philo, the motivation for sexual intercourse must never be pleasure or else it is unnatural, and this is true even within the marriage relationship. He asserts that a man should keep track of his wife's menstrual cycle and never approach her sexually if she is not in a fertile time. In his philosophical view, a man must never waste his "generative seeds" (that is, sperm) "for the sake of gross and untimely pleasure."[15] Comparing the woman to a field, Philo says that a man must watch his wife carefully in order to determine when she is productive and ready for him to sow his seed into her. Consequently, having sex with a barren wife is sinful because it constitutes willful destruction of generative seeds. Philo is willing to pardon a man who does not want to divorce his wife when he discovers after several years of marriage that she is barren, but anyone who marries a woman who is proven to be barren by a former marriage he compares to someone who copulates like a pig or a goat. Such a man is an enemy of God, for God created sex to lead to reproduction, and the man who makes love to his wife as a mere expression of passionate desire is an enemy of nature.[16]

With this great concern to uphold what he views as natural, Philo is understandably very disturbed over the widespread occurrence of homosexuality in the Greco-Roman world:

> In former days the very mention of it was a great disgrace, but now it is a matter of boasting not only to the active but to the passive partners, who habituate themselves to endure the disease of effemination, let both body and soul run to waste, and leave no ember of their male sex-nature to smoulder. Mark how conspicuously they braid and adorn the hair of their heads, and how they scrub and paint their faces with cosmetics and pigments and the like, and smother themselves with fragrant unguents. . . . the transformation of the male nature to the female is practised by them as an art and does not raise a blush.[17]

He goes on to assert that such men who have debased their male sex natures are a disgrace to themselves, their families, their homelands, and the entire human race. And a man who plays the active role with a "man-woman" is a terrible "instructor in the grievous vices of unmanliness and effeminacy by prolonging the bloom of the young and emasculating the flower of their prime, which should rightly be trained to strength and robustness."[18]

Although Philo would agree with Paul on the basis of human anatomy that homosexuality is against nature, his understanding of the natural function of sex is quite different. Paul's view of marital intercourse is much the same as that which we saw in Deuteronomy, Proverbs, and the Song of Songs, namely that sex is an enjoyable part of marriage and is not merely for the purpose of propagating the human race. Philo's insistence that sex is only natural when reproduction is in mind owes virtually nothing to his Jewish heritage. His teaching reflects his assimilation of Greek philosophical thinking, and we may legitimately ask how much of his Jewish heritage he destroyed in his attempt to defend it. By seeking to make Judaism credible to the Greco-Roman world, he often forced the Old Testament to espouse the philosophical and scientific views of his day that he deemed most respectable.

When we reflect upon Philo's dilemma, it is not difficult to understand the tension he faced. On the one hand he was a highly educated man who found his intellectual life in conflict with a literal understanding of the Old Testament. His Scriptures did not openly

support the educated world views of his time, and he was convinced of the validity of much of what he learned from contemporary philosophy and science. On the other hand he believed that the Hebrew Scriptures were God's gift to the Jewish people; and, therefore, since the Scriptures were divine in origin, they must in fact represent the truth in everything. How could he reconcile his faith commitment with his intellectual contemplation? He adopted allegory as his dominant method of interpreting the Scriptures, and as a result he was able to resolve the conflict between science and faith.

Through allegorical interpretation Philo could look for deeper, "spiritual" meanings that would be very compatible with his own "modern" understanding of reality. Also, this same method enabled him to eliminate elements of the Scriptures that he deemed to be offensive, such as those passages attributing qualities or actions to God that Philo simply could not accept as being literally true. Consequently, he affirmed his own brand of Judaized Greco-Roman philosophy and philosophized Judaism. This intermixing is apparent in his views on the natural function of sex, for he holds to an intensified Jewish morality over against the lower sexual standards of most of the Greco-Roman world; yet he excludes the usual Jewish affirmation of the enjoyable nature of sexual relations within marriage. Philo's belief in the perverse nature of homosexuality is in line with other first-century Jewish writers, including the Apostle Paul, although his explanation of the phenomenon is different. Theirs was a minority view, however, since the majority of the people in the Greco-Roman world did not label it as unnatural.

Greco–Roman Acceptance of Homosexuality

Unlike the Jewish aversion to homosexuality maintained by Paul, the Greeks and Romans for the most part seem to have accepted it as a *natural* expression of affection, at least among men. There were, however, certain ethical codes for the practice of physical love between

males, and distinctions were made between the types of men who engaged in these activities. There were effeminate types such as the ones Philo disgustedly described, who took great pains with their physical appearance and retained few "manly" attributes. Such males could be found, for example, in the households of wealthy men who took special delight in supporting them. Society as a whole tended to view these effeminates with a certain amount of disdain. On the other hand, it was common for men who were very masculine to engage in sexual encounters with each other, and society viewed this as normal. For these men the term *homosexual* is actually not as accurate as *bisexual*, for their relations with men were not exclusive. Sex was simply a very normal part of existence; and a man might have a wife and children, visit *hetairai* (the female companions described in the chapter on 1 Corinthians), and have several male lovers all at the same time.

In Greek culture there are numerous indications that for centuries before the time of Paul it was common for men to have male lovers, and this practice was considered noble and chaste when performed correctly. This viewpoint is given elegant expression by a certain Phaedrus, one of the characters in Plato's Symposium. *His speech* is primarily devoted to the noble love of men for each other, and therefore it has a great deal of relevance to our topic. Appealing to the legends recorded by famous Greek poets, Phaedrus claims that Love is an unbegotten god whose existence predates that of most of the other deities. Then in exalted words of praise, he extols the virtues brought about by the mutual love between a more mature man, whom he calls a lover, and a younger male, whom he calls either a favorite or a beloved. It is hard to imagine a greater contrast with the Apostle Paul's view of homosexual relations as debauched perversity than the following eulogy of the same:

> Thus Love is by various authorities allowed to be of most venerable standing; and as most venerable, he is the cause of all our highest blessings. I for my part am at a loss to say what greater blessing a man can have in earliest youth than an honourable lover, or a lover than an honourable favourite. For the guiding principle we should choose for all our days, if we are minded to live a comely life, cannot be acquired

either by kinship or office or wealth or anything so well as by Love. What shall I call this power? The shame that we feel for shameful things, and ambition for what is noble; without which it is impossible for city or person to perform any high and noble deeds. Let me then say that a man in love, should he be detected in some shameful act or in a cowardly submission to shameful treatment at another's hands, would not feel half so much distress at anyone observing it, whether father or comrade or anyone in the world, as when his favourite did; and in the selfsame way we see how the beloved is especially ashamed before his lovers when he is observed to be about some shameful business. So that if we could somewise contrive to have a city or an army composed of lovers and their favourites, they could not be better citizens of their country than by thus refraining from all that is base in a mutual rivalry for honour; and such men as these, when fighting side by side, one might almost consider able to make even a little band victorious over all the world. For a man in love would surely choose to have all the rest of the host rather than his favourite see him forsaking his station or flinging away his arms; sooner than this, he would prefer to die many deaths: while, as for leaving his favourite in the lurch, or not succouring him in his peril, no man is such a craven that Love's own influence cannot inspire him with a valour that makes him equal to the bravest born; and without doubt what Homer calls a 'fury inspired' by a god in certain heroes is the effect produced on lovers by Love's peculiar power.

. . . For in truth there is no sort of valour more respected by the gods than this which comes of love; yet they are even more admiring and delighted and beneficent when the beloved is fond of his lover than when the lover is fond of his favourite; since a lover, filled as he is with a god, surpasses his favourite in divinity.[19]

The "lover" in Phaedrus' speech, a mature man who has devoted special attention to a boy, shared more with the youth than just sexual relations. In such relationships the man often considered it his duty to train his beloved boy in the ways of virtue, leading him toward excellence in bravery as a warrior, wisdom in the conduct of everyday affairs of life, and responsibility as a citizen. Thus, these homosexual relationships were viewed by Greek societies as valuable educational experiences for boys who were fortunate enough to be courted by noble men.

Within Greek culture it was a common practice for mature men to be greatly attracted to the beauty of boys who had reached the age of

puberty.[20] Expending considerable energy in courting boys, these men would exhibit emotions of infatuation and jealousy as they vied with one another for the affections of the boys. There are examples in ancient Greek literature of love poems written by men for boys, poetry containing descriptions of beauty and personal passion that most people would expect a man to write about a beautiful woman.[21] Even the great philosopher Socrates participated in the activity of pursuing youth, as is attested by the opening lines of Plato's *Protagorus*:

> FRIEND: Where have you come from, Socrates? No doubt from pursuit of the captivating Alcibiades. Certainly when I saw him only a day or two ago, he seemed to be still a handsome man; but between ourselves, Socrates, "man" is the word. He's actually growing a beard.
>
> SOCRATES: What of it? Aren't you an enthusiast for Homer, who says that the most charming age is that of the youth with his first beard, just the age of Alcibiades now?
>
> FRIEND: Well what's the news? Have you just left the young man, and how is he disposed towards you?
>
> SOCRATES: Very well, I think, . . . as you guessed, I have only just left him. But I will tell you a surprising thing: although he was present, I had no thought for him, and often forgot him altogether.
>
> FRIEND: Why, what can have happened between you and him to make such a difference? You surely can't have met someone more handsome—not in Athens at least?[22]

The great emphasis on the beauty of the young male, so evident in the artwork of the Greeks, is celebrated on numerous occasions in their literature as well. Xenophon (c. 430–355 B.C.), a contemporary of Plato (437?–347 B.C.), provides a revealing description of the reactions of the men at a banquet when a handsome youth entered: "Just as the sudden glow of a light draws all eyes to itself, so now the beauty of Autolycus compelled everyone to look at him. And again, there was not one of the onlookers who did not feel his soul strangely stirred by the boy."[23] Xenophon describes a reverent hush that descended on the banquet as they beheld the godlike form; and later, when a youth plays his lyre and sings, one of the men states, "It seems to me, gentlemen,

that, as Socrates said of the wine, so this blending of the young people's beauty and of the notes of the music . . . awakens the goddess of love."[24]

In Xenophon's *Memorabilia* is a description of Socrates instructing one of his students in the art of obtaining male lovers:

> Courage, Critobulus; try to be good, and when you have achieved that, set about catching your gentlemen. Maybe, I myself, as an adept in love, can lend you a hand in the pursuit of gentlemen. For when I want to catch anyone it's surprising how I strain every nerve to have my love returned . . . that he shall want me as much as I want him. I see that you too will feel this need when you want to form a friendship. So do not hide from me the names of those whom you wish to make your friends; for I am careful to please him who pleases me, and so, I think, I am not without experience in the pursuit of men.[25]

Socrates then proceeds to give advice to Critobulus on the art of catching men.[26] Unabashed accounts of this kind illustrate the vast difference in thinking between Paul and much of the Greek world concerning what is natural and unnatural. Whereas the Greeks could claim divine pleasure upon homosexual relations, Paul asserts strongly in Romans 1 that the very existence of such perversity is evidence of divine wrath.

Homosexual relations between men in Greece were considered ignoble only if money was the reason for the activity. Aristophanes (c. 448–380 B.C.) speaks of baser type boys who sell their love for money,[27] and Aeschines (c. 390 B.C.–?) records in this regard the charges leveled against a certain Timarchus, who was seeking a public office. Among other things, Timarchus was accused of selling himself as a youth, an action considered shameful.[28] Specifically the charge is that he "lived to the shame of his own body and of the city, earning wages by precisely that thing which the law forbids."[29] Timarchus defends himself by citing an example of the fidelity of two heroes, Harmodius and Aristogeiton, whose "relationship proved to be the salvation of the state,"[30] and he adds that the friendship of the heroes in Homer, Patroclus and Achilles, "had its source in passion."[31] Although admitting that infatuation with and passion toward young boys can cause strife among men,[32] in his defense Timarchus states,

> I neither find fault with love that is honourable. . . . I do not deny that
> I myself have been a lover and am a lover to this day, nor do I deny that
> the jealousies and quarrels that commonly arise from the practice have
> happened in my case. . . . The distinction which I draw is this: to be in
> love with those who are beautiful and chaste is the experience of a
> kind-hearted and generous soul; but to hire for money and to indulge in
> licentiousness is the act of a man who is wanton and ill-bred. And
> whereas it is an honour to be the object of a pure love, I declare that he
> who has played the prostitute by inducement of wages is disgraced.[33]

Timarchus then goes on to say that the great Greek lawgivers did not
think that a boy was harmed by these affairs, "but rather that such a
thing was a testimony to his chastity."[34] Nevertheless, he adds that a
man should be careful not to woo a boy who is not yet old enough to
determine if a man is a true or a false friend.[35] Thus, whereas Paul calls
all homosexuality perverse and against nature, Timarchus distinguishes
between what he calls beautiful and chaste male-to-male love and
licentious male love for money.

The ancient Greek custom of men taking boy lovers continued to
be a common practice well past the time Paul wrote his epistle to the
Roman church. It was not limited to the Greek culture either, for
there are numerous indications in Roman artwork and literature that
their men engaged in these same activities.[36] The dominant sentiment
in Greco-Roman culture appears to have been very accepting of
homosexuality as long as it was not a dominating preoccupation, for
having male lovers seems seldom to have excluded relations with women. Socrates, for example, according to Xenophon, had a faithful
wife, male lovers, and also visited female friends other than his wife.[37]

The second-century-A.D. satirist Lucian, in his *Amores* 53, describes the sequence he likes to follow when he desires sexual contact
with a beloved boy. In very explicit language he explains how he
progresses from a light touch to a light kiss and on to consummation.
After his description he states,

> May I for my part find it my lot to love boys in this way. But may the
> airy talkers and those who raise their philosophic brows temple-high
> and even higher, beguile the ignorant with the speciousness of their
> solemn phrases. For Socrates was as devoted to love as anyone and

Alcibiades, once he had lain down beneath the same mantle with him, did not rise unassailed.[38] Don't be surprised at that. For not even the affection of Achilles for Patroclus was limited to having him seated opposite. . . . No, pleasure was the mediator even of *their* friendship. At any rate, when Achilles was lamenting the death of Patroclus, his unrestrained feelings made him burst out with the truth and say, "The converse of our thighs my tears do mourn. . . ."[39]

Lucian's reference to certain philosophers who disapprove of men chasing boys is an indication that not everyone in his culture saw the practice as harmless. Nevertheless, the limited number of extant Greek and Roman writings that condemn homosexuality seems to indicate that the number of its opponents was not great. Apparently very few would have nodded in agreement if they had read Paul's opinion in Rom. 1:18–32.

Actually, in the Greco-Roman world effeminate practices appear to have been the greater cause of concern. If homosexual relations caused a man to become effeminate, there would be much more likelihood of arousing criticism than if two very masculine types loved each other. For example, the first-century-A.D. Stoic philosopher Epictetus harshly criticized men who altered their masculinity. In one of his discourses he disdainfully speaks of a situation wherein some women were expressing preference for men with smooth skin, and so some of the young men were plucking the hair out of their legs in order to please the women. Epictetus sarcastically asserts that if women like smooth men, it is just too bad, and his rationale is intriguing. A man should never go against his *own nature* to please a woman, for a man is beautiful only when he fulfills what he is *by nature*:

Are you a man or a woman?—A man.—Very well then, adorn a man, not a woman. Woman is born smooth and dainty by nature. . . . Man, what reason have you to complain against your nature. . . . Your paltry body doesn't please you, eh? Make a clean sweep of the whole matter; eradicate your—what shall I call it?—the cause of your hairiness; make yourself a woman all over, so as not to deceive us, not half-man and half-woman. Whom do you wish to please? Frail womankind? Please them as a man. "Yes, but they like smooth men." Oh, go hang! And if they liked sexual perverts, would you have become such a pervert? Is

> this your business in life . . . that licentious women should take plea-
> sure in you? Shall we make a man like you a citizen of Corinth . . .?
>
> . . . Come then, let us obey God, that we rest not under his
> wrath. . . . But observe what Socrates says to Alcibiades. . . . What
> does he tell him? "Dress your locks and pluck the hairs out of your
> legs?" God forbid![40]

Epictetus reveals a strong concern for natural order, and his sarcastic
comment about Corinth is further evidence for the bad reputation of
that city for vice. In words reminiscent of Paul, he states that God's
wrath is upon those who go against nature, and his concluding "God
forbid!" is one of Paul's favorite ways of expressing a definite no to a
rhetorical question (Greek, *mē genoito*; for example, Rom. 6:1–2, 15;
7:7). As a Stoic philosopher, Epictetus' theological rationale for his
statements differed from Paul's, yet his moral philosophy is one example that illustrates that argumentation based on natural order was not
uncommon during the first century. What was uncommon for non-
Jews was to call homosexuality unnatural.

When Plutarch (c. A.D. 46–120) gives his account of the way
young men were formerly trained at Sparta, he describes homosexuality
among them in very positive terms, since it produced masculinity. He
says that at twelve years of age the boys "were favoured with the society
of lovers from among the reputable young men,"[41] who trained them
in virtue.

> The boys' lovers also shared with them in their honour or disgrace; and
> it is said that one of them was once fined by the magistrates because his
> favourite boy had let an ungenerous cry escape him while he was fight-
> ing. Moreover, this sort of love was so approved among them that even
> the maidens found lovers in good and noble women, still, there was no
> jealous rivalry in it, but those who fixed their affections on the same
> boys made this rather a foundation for friendship with one another, and
> persevered in common efforts to make their loved one as noble as possi-
> ble.[42]

On the one hand, Plutarch's glowing account is obviously rather over-
done, but on the other hand it vividly illustrates the fact that he makes
no censure of Spartan practices in this matter.

Some of the Greek and Roman writers did censure lesbianism, however, and their complaint seems to be that one of the women must play the male role, which is "unnatural." Oddly enough, this argument, although equally applicable to male homosexual relations, does not appear to have been used by these same authors. Martial, a first-century-A.D. Roman writer, speaks of a woman who was never intimate with men but always was with women. Critically he says, "You dare things unspeakable, and your portentious lust imitates man."[43] In a similar vein, Lucian tells of a certain Clorarium asking another woman, Leaena, if it is true that she is having lesbian relations with a certain rich woman. Leaena responds, "Quite true, Clorarium. But I'm ashamed, for it's unnatural."[44] The meaning of *unnatural* is obvious from the way she describes the rich woman as being very much like a man—like some woman in Lesbos—as well as her admission that the woman told her, "I was born a woman like the rest of you, but I have the mind and the desires and everything else of a man."[45]

Thus, it appears that in the Greco-Roman world lesbianism would have received more censure than male-to-male relations. The greatest concern, however, was with men and women denying their own natures and a man becoming effeminate or a woman becoming masculine. This understanding of what is "natural," although having certain similarities with Paul's view of what is against nature in Rom. 1:26–27, has obvious dissimilarities also. For Paul the homosexual act itself was perverted and unnatural and therefore degrading to the body. For the Greeks and Romans the sex act was typically not so much the concern as was the question of a person's masculinity or femininity.

Conclusions

The Greco-Roman world of Paul's time was for the most part tolerant of homosexual relations among men, although lesbian relations were frequently viewed with suspicion or animosity. Typically the fact that a man had male lovers did not at all mean that he did not also have a wife and children. Neither did it mean that the man was effeminate, for many of the most valiant soldiers had lovers who were also very rugged

and brave types. For the Greek and Roman men, at least, sex was simply not as restricted as it was among the Jewish people. There were certainly those among the Romans who decried the disintegration of the family structure in Roman society, and there were attempts made to correct the moral decline. But the sexual standards of the Greco-Roman culture were generally far less confining than those of the Jews. As long as homosexual relations did not cause a man to exhibit effeminate tendencies, or to become truly "homosexual" instead of merely bisexual in orientation, they were generally not considered perverse.

Among the Jews, however, homosexuality was considered a perversion that violated the order God had created. Often calling it the sin of Sodom, in reference to Genesis 19, most Jewish writers believed that such behavior was terribly repugnant to God, who would one day come in wrath to judge those who practiced it. The Apostle Paul's view of homosexuality was essentially the same as that expressed by Jewish authors, except that he added a unique observation. Paul believed that the very existence of homosexuality was proof that God's wrath was already being shown toward people. In Paul's mind homosexuality was so demeaning that the practice itself was to be explained as resulting from God's turning people loose to debase themselves. Because they had rejected God and refused to worship him, choosing to serve idols instead, God delivered them in their confused and darkened minds to accomplish all sorts of perversity. Confused about God, the Gentiles also became confused about themselves, becoming less than human because they insisted on worshipping something less than God. By abandoning their Creator, they were also abandoned by him; and, in their abandoned state, their thinking became so darkened that they exchanged the natural function of sexual intercourse between male and female for the unnatural relations of men with men and women with women.

Paul's statements about homosexuality in Rom. 1:18–32 were not written as a special attack on this practice, however, but as an extreme example of Gentile perversity. He used it as part of his larger argument of Rom. 1–3: that *all* are guilty before God and in need of forgiveness and salvation through faith in Christ. Homosexuality was

for Paul but one example of Gentile immorality, yet it was his best illustration for effectively arguing his point. According to Paul, Gentiles who practice homosexuality and the other vices he lists in Rom. 1:29–31 are guilty of sin; and Jews, who detest Gentile idolatry and immorality, are also guilty because they have broken the law of God (2:17–29). Both Jew and Gentile have fallen short of God's righteousness, and both need God's grace. Paul's message in Romans is very clear: God offers a new life to every person who will receive the salvation he offers as a free gift. In Rom. 1–3 he seeks to establish the reality of universal bondage; in Rom. 4–15 he seeks to lead people into a full understanding of liberty in Christ.

Notes

1. Trans. R. H. Charles, ed., *The Apocrypha and Pseudepigrapha of the Old Testament in English*, vol. II (Oxford, Eng.: Clarendon Press, 1913), p. 262.

2. Cf. 1 Thessalonians 1:10; 2:16; 5:9.

3. T. Levi 17:11, trans. Charles, ed., *Pseudepigrapha*, p. 314.

4. T. Naphtali 4:1; cf. T. Benjamin 9:1. Ibid., p. 337.

5. T. Naphtali 3:2–4. Ibid., p. 337. Although dating the final collection of the T. of the 12 Patriarchs is problematic, the discovery of a Hebrew fragment of the T. Naphtali at Qumran shows that this text was written by a Jewish author prior to Paul. See Leonhard Rost, *Judiasm Outside the Hebrew Canon: An Introduction to the Documents*, trans. David E. Green (Nashville: Abingdon, 1976), pp. 144–45.

6. The Jewish Sibylline Oracles argue that God revealed himself through his creation, but the Romans worship animals and idols instead of God (Bk. III. 8–35; cf. V 278–79). The oracles rebuke the Romans for such idol worship, which ignores God's self-revelation in nature (Bk. IV. 8, 10, 12; Fragment i. 25–28; ii. 22–23, 27–31), and they accuse them of foully abusing boys (Bk. V. 166–67, 387–93; see also III. 185–86; IV. 33–34). Oracle V. 430 calls passion for boys "unnatural."

7. Trans. Charles, ed., *Pseudepigrapha*, p. 389.

8. Ibid., p. 435.

9. *On Abraham* 134, trans. F. H. Colson, *Philo*, vol. VI, the Loeb Classical Library (Cambridge, Mass.: Harvard University Press, 1935), p. 71.

10. *On Abraham* 135. Ibid.

11. Ibid.

12. *On Abraham* 136. Ibid.

13. *On Abraham* 137. Ibid.

14. *The Special Laws* II.50, trans. F. H. Colson, *Philo*, vol. VII, the Loeb Classical Library (Cambridge, Mass.: Harvard University Press, 1937), p. 339.

15. *Special Laws* III.32. Ibid., p. 495.

16. *Special Laws* III.32–36.

17. *Special Laws* III.37. Ibid., p. 499.

18. *Special Laws* III.39. Ibid., pp. 499, 501.

19. *Symposium* 178c–179b, 180a, trans. W. R. M. Lamb, *Plato*, vol. V, the Loeb Classical Library (New York: G. P. Putnam's Sons, 1925), pp. 101, 103, 107.

20. Hans Licht, *Sexual Life in Ancient Greece* (New York: Barnes & Noble, Inc., 1963), pp. 419–27, provides numerous examples of Greek appreciation for the beauty of young males.

21. Ibid., pp. 427–30.

22. *Protagorus* 309a–c, trans. W. K. C. Guthrie, *Protagorus and Meno*, The Penguin Classics (Baltimore: Penguin Books, 1956), p. 38. Reprinted by permission of Penguin Books Ltd.

23. *Symposium* I.9, trans. O. J. Todd, *Xenophon: Anabasis, Books IV–VII and Symposium and Apology*, the Loeb Classical Library (Cambridge, Mass.: Harvard University Press, 1922), p. 383.

24. *Symposium* III.1. Ibid., p. 403.

25. *Memorabilia* II.vi.28–29. Trans. E. C. Marchant, *Xenophon: Memorabilia and Oeconomicus*, the Loeb Classical Library (Cambridge, Mass.: Harvard University Press, 1923), p. 141.

26. *Memorabilia* II.vi.30–39.

27. *The Plutus* 153.

28. *Against Timarchus* 29–30.

29. *Against Timarchus* 40, trans. Charles Darwin Adams, *The Speeches of Aeschines*, the Loeb Classical Library (New York: G. P. Putnam's Sons, 1919), p. 37.

30. *Against Timarchus* 132. Ibid., p. 107.

31. *Against Timarchus* 133. Ibid., p. 109.

32. *Against Timarchus* 134. Ibid.

33. *Against Timarchus* 136–37. Ibid., p. 111.

34. *Against Timarchus* 139. Ibid., p. 113.

35. *Against Timarchus* 139–40. (cf. §12, which records a law that strictly forbids men from entering the schools of young boys. Such behavior was considered "seduction of a free-born youth" and carried the death penalty. §13 provides information on a law that prosecutes anyone who sells or hires a boy for sexual purposes).

36. See any of the pictorial books on ancient Roman art, especially on Pompey. See also Otto Kieffer, *Sexual Life in Ancient Rome* (London: Routledge & Kegan Paul Ltd., 1934), pp. 151–52, 165.

37. *Memorabilia* III.xi.1–18.

38. This is a contradiction of Plato's version of the story in *Symposium* 218c–219e, where Alcibiades tries to seduce Socrates but Socrates exhibits amazing self-control.

39. *Amores* 54, trans. M. D. Macleod, *Lucian*, vol. VIII, the Loeb Classical Library (Cambridge, Mass.: Harvard University Press, 1967), pp. 233–34.

40. *Discourses* III.1:27, 29, 31–34, 37, 42–44, trans. W. A. Oldfather, *Epictetus: The Discourses as Reported by Arrian, the Manual, and Fragments*, vol. II, the Loeb Classical Library (New York: G. P. Putnam's Sons, 1928), pp. 15, 17, 19, 21.

41. *Lycurgus* XVII. 1, trans. Bernadotte Perrin, *Plutarch's Lives*, vol. I, the Loeb Classical Library (New York: The Macmillan Co., 1914), p. 259.

42. *Lycurgus* XVIII.4. Ibid., pp. 263, 265.

43. *Epigrams* I.90, trans. Walter C. A. Ker, *Martial: Epigrams*, vol. I, the Loeb Classical Library (New York: G. P. Putnam's Sons, 1919), p. 87.

44. *Dialogues of the Courtesans* 5, "Leaena and Clorarium," §289, trans. M. D. Macleod, *Lucian*, vol. VII, the Loeb Classical Library (Cambridge, Mass.: Harvard University Press, 1961), p. 381.

45. Ibid., §292, p. 385.

Modern Sexuality and Biblical Perspectives

Throughout this book our goal has been to gain a deeper understanding of selected biblical material. Not being content to observe merely *what* the documents say about matters pertaining to sex and marriage, we have sought to determine *why* they say these things. We would fall short of completing our task, however, if we failed to consider the relevance of the Bible for our thinking today on these matters.

The frequently severe laws of Deuteronomy reflect the conditions of a culture vastly different from our own, and it would be impossible to implement many of them today. Regulations pertaining to such topics as the taking of female captives for wives or slaves and the levirate marriage are part of a remote past. Although some laws have perennial relevance, such as prohibitions against murder and theft, a great number of laws in any society reflect the existing conditions of the time and would have little or no relevance beyond their own societal context. Laws continually evolve as new conditions develop; and as new legislation emerges, many old laws become obsolete and must be abandoned or modified. In the modern world, with international corporations and air traffic between various countries, imagine how senseless it would be to maintain nineteenth-century regulations

on tying horses to hitching racks while in town! The only relevance these old laws would have for us today would be that we can observe how they were meant to protect people and their property from being harmed. Similarly, laws in Deuteronomy concerning the bride price, or the inheritance of the firstborn son in a polygamous marriage, or forcing a rapist to marry the woman he raped are irrelevant today. Such regulations are foreign to our culture, and it would be disastrous to try to implement them. Only some of the principles that undergird these laws have abiding relevance.

We may therefore benefit by focusing on why the laws of Deuteronomy were written, even though actually adopting them ourselves would be rather ridiculous. For example, in light of the tremendous advances made by women in the recent past in the area of equal rights, the Deuteronomic laws pertaining to women now appear to be extremely demeaning. By modern standards this is certainly true, but by ancient standards some of these laws were designed to protect women from exploitation. With the almost total male dominance of the Hebrew culture of that time, when women were owned by the men, some Mosaic legislation sought to prevent men from abusing the power they possessed over the women. What sounds inconsiderate to us today actually was compassionate then. How ironic it would be if we were to take an ancient law that was originally intended to prevent women from being oppressed and seek to use it today, when its very implementation would oppress women!

Perhaps it is much easier for many people to see the contemporary relevance of the principles taught in Proverbs than in the laws of Deuteronomy. Although total adoption of the Wisdom School's understanding of the nature of the cosmos is not necessarily desirable, contemplation of some of their major emphases is extremely beneficial. For example, Prov. 1–7 stresses the importance of viewing each individual action in light of life as a whole. In the realm of sexual ethics, the sages assert that wisdom allows a person to see that what may look extremely attractive and enticing may in fact be death producing. For people today, who are continually bombarded with mass-media messages affirming the delights of casual sexual encounters, the seduction scene of

Prov. 7:6–27 has particular relevance. In this story of an adulterous woman enticing a young man to enjoy a free night of feasting and sexual adventure, there is a powerful magnetism in her seductive appeal. Yet the writer of the story warns that behind the outwardly attractive appearance lies the miserable reality of the true consequences of adultery. From the perspective of Proverbs, therefore, the smiles of lovely Hollywood faces hide the grim reality of the destructive sexual ethics so often proclaimed by the silver screen. The beautiful bedroom doors and laughing actors and actresses conceal the life-destroying realities involved in such experiences. The thrill of one night is in no way worth the lifelong guilty conscience of knowing that you were unfaithful to your husband or wife, nor is it worth the chance of contracting venereal disease.

Instead of legislating morality, Proverbs seeks to help us think through the benefits of living morally: Not only is it right to do so, but it is also best. In the long run, those who live moral lives will be those who will experience the most joy in life. Thus Prov. 5:15–19 advises a man to delight himself so much in his own wife that he gains contentment with her. By focusing on her good attributes and seeking to enjoy life with her, including a passionate sex life, he will not be concerned to look elsewhere and contemplate whether other women are more desirable. Contentment in marriage may be gained through living wisely.

Many contemporary conditions are in no way addressed by Proverbs, yet the Wisdom approach to life would certainly aid in grappling with these issues. Since the sages sought to understand life by careful observation of how things work in the total system of the cosmos, their endeavor is by nature open to modification. For example, in their culture having an abundance of children was very desirable, and birth control would not have been an issue of concern. They considered it wise to have many children. Today, however, with overpopulation being a tremendous problem that produces immense human suffering and ecological devastation, the same Wisdom approach to life would consider birth control to be very wise. Conditions change with the passage of time, and what is wise in one era may be foolish in

another. Wisdom helps us to determine which things are *timeless* and which are only *timely*.

For example, in ancient Hebrew culture, where people married at a very early age, there was not as great a problem with sexual frustration caused by extended single life. But what advice would a modern sage give to a twenty-five-year-old man or woman who is unmarried and struggling terribly with sexual desire? Virtually everywhere such people look, they see what amounts to a mass campaign to stimulate them. On billboards the men see seductively dressed, voluptuous women advertising—Sex. A vast number of movies and TV shows joke about, talk about, or even show Sex, or at least some foreplay. Magazine and book racks are full of pictures and stories about Sex. What advice can a wise educator of youth give to those who live in a culture where Sex is exploited to sell everything from toothpaste to cars, and the bodies of handsome men and beautiful women are offered in commercial sacrifice upon the altar of the god Sex? Is it inevitable that people must be forced, by the sheer power of the media campaign, to fall down and worship this deity?

Modern sages must reckon with contemporary problems and offer timely advice and penetrating insights. For example, as they observe the insecurity and unhappiness that often results when people look despairingly into mirrors, wondering why they do not have the beauty of movie stars, the sages need to reflect upon the place of physical beauty in our culture. Ironically, this mistaken notion that happiness in life is equated with beauty also negatively affects those who are exceptionally good-looking. Many very attractive men and women are among the most unhappy people in our culture, often because they are tired of being viewed as objects instead of persons or because they have not yet truly realized that physical beauty has little to do with authentic participation in life.[1] So the sage must wisely consider these factors and ponder over what brings deep contentment in life. Then he or she must reason with those who are constantly tempted to go to the temple of Sex and help them to understand that sex is just a part of creation, not a deity. To worship it is to diminish its value. Such idolatry does not lead to full human joy but results instead in dehumanization and its

accompanying misery (cf. Rom. 1:18–32). It is the antithesis of Jesus' teaching.

In the Synoptic Gospel accounts of Jesus, we once again encounter the divine command ("thus says the Lord!") which we saw in Deuteronomy, yet his words are not those of a law code. Speaking with prophetic forcefulness, Jesus sought not to formulate laws for virtually every aspect of life but to provide a rationale for how to live life as a whole. He offered compassionate forgiveness and a new life for sexual offenders, giving them an opportunity to leave behind the mistakes of the past and make a fresh beginning. Offering life to replace the deadly consequences brought about by their former actions, Jesus attracted to himself a large number of people who were burdened by guilt. To those who felt helpless in coping with their present situations or correcting conditions that had resulted from previous mistakes, he gave new hope. Men and women struggling through the negative effects brought about by fornication, divorce, prostitution, and so on, could gain a new freedom through sincerely repenting and embracing Jesus' proclamation of the kingdom of God and his law of love. By coming to Jesus, such people not only gained a new direction in life, but through experiencing forgiveness they could be freed from the spiritual and psychological bondage of guilt and regret.

From Jesus' viewpoint, all of life should be governed by a deep love for God and other people. Instead of determining what to do in each of our many daily decisions by reflecting upon what is required by some law, Jesus would have us ask, "What is the most ethical and loving thing I could do in this situation?" His focus was upon what is right, not upon what is legal. The question for him was not: "What can I get away with in order to gratify my own desires?" but "How can I best serve God and give of myself to help others?"

Jesus' teaching on a life-style of love in total obedience to God resulted in an interesting combination of respect for Old Testament law and a readiness to modify it. On the one hand his moral code was very much that of Judaism, and he affirmed that sex should be limited to the marriage relationship. On the other hand, he intensified the demands for moral purity, asserting that God is concerned about a per-

son's thought life as well as his or her overt actions. Piety must be without hypocrisy, based on a thorough commitment to live a life of total sincerity. Thus, if we were to make the seduction story of Prov. 7:6–27 even more enticing by saying that the woman was "beautiful" and "gracious" and that there was "absolutely no chance" of suffering any negative social consequences from spending the night with her, what would Jesus say? "No matter how tempting or how safe an action may be, if it is wrong, it is wrong and should not be done."

In a modern setting we could rephrase the issue as follows: What if you are a man on a business venture to a distant city, perhaps even in another country. You are all alone on the trip, you know no one in the city, and tomorrow you will continue on to yet another city. What if a beautiful woman who is eating alone at a table near you in a restaurant initiates a conversation with you, admits that she is very lonely, and invites you to spend the night with her. You will never see her again, and neither your wife nor anyone else would ever have any way of finding out. What would you do? Or if we changed the characters of the story around to portray a businesswoman on a trip who meets a handsome man in a restaurant, what would you do? From Jesus' perspective, you would not even have to calculate the pros and cons in order to reach a decision. God would know; you would know; and the action is wrong. Therefore you would choose what is right because it is right. To be unfaithful to your wife or husband is against God's will and is not a loving action toward either your mate or the attractive person in the distant city.

Jesus' teaching on love and moral purity led him to modify parts of the Mosaic law. Whereas Deuteronomy 24:1–4 considers divorce to be the husband's right, Jesus asserts that a man does not have the "right" to divorce his wife. As a matter of fact, in Mark's account Jesus actually states that some of the Old Testament laws were given by God as concessions to human evil and do not represent his true will for people: "Jesus said to them, 'He wrote this command because of your hard heart. . . . What therefore God has joined together, man must not separate! . . . Whoever divorces his wife and marries another commits adultery against her; and if she divorces her husband to marry

another, she commits adultery' " (Mark 10:5, 9, 11–12). What is "legal" under Mosaic law concerning divorce is not acceptable in Jesus' prophetic proclamation of what is "best." God only allowed divorce because of human evil; and to live life fully as God intended, men and women must give up their "right" to divorce. Granted, situations can and do arise in which divorce is permissible, but according to Jesus this is not in accord with God's ideal standard for people. Undoubtedly a great deal of the suffering experienced by men and women and their children when divorces occur could be averted if husbands and wives would make Jesus' law of love the basis for their lives.

Concerning the issue of celibacy, Jesus not only called it a perfectly acceptable option, but he himself remained single. For those who desired to be free from the responsibilities involved in a marriage relationship so that they could concentrate more intensely on building the kingdom of God, Jesus pronounced freedom from the normally expected Jewish "duty" to marry and have children. Thus single people are not somehow incomplete as persons, and they do not have a second-class status as citizens of the kingdom of God. The Apostle Paul, for example, was one of those who chose this option to remain celibate.

Paul expected Jesus Christ to return to earth very soon and bring an end to the present age. In light of this belief he counseled those Christians at Corinth who were not married to remain single, for he thought that times were going to become difficult in the near future and that marriage would increase the difficulty of coping with the stress. Paul therefore regarded celibacy as more desirable than marriage due to the expected advent of the Messianic Woes, but he evidently did not believe that marriage was a mere second-best option. For him the question every Christian must answer is, What is God's will for my life? Had he known that Jesus was actually not going to return in the very near future, he would have given different advice in 1 Cor. 7 to the engaged couples at Corinth.

According to Paul, all of life should be lived in obedience to the will of God: "Therefore whether you eat or drink or whatever else you do, do everything for the glory of God" (1 Cor. 10:31). Fully in

agreement with Jesus' law of love, he taught Christians that they should not merely do what was required by law, but that through love they must learn to go beyond questions of legality, even when this meant personal sacrifice.

Morally speaking, Paul held strongly to the sexual ethics of his Jewish ancestry: Sex is legitimate only within marriage. Standing in opposition to the popular morality of the Greco-Roman world, he insisted that Christians must maintain moral purity. He viewed adultery, premarital sex, homosexual acts, and so on as sinful and asserted that those who practice these things are under the wrath of God. To all such people he extended the good news (or Gospel) of forgiveness of sins through faith in the sacrificial death of Jesus Christ. The invitation was open to all, and Paul's message was clear: Only by receiving the free gift of God's grace through faith in Christ can a person be righteous and enjoy a full relationship with God. To be liberated from bondage to selfish and perverted living, each person must therefore experience this purifying encounter with God.

With forceful clarity the teachings of Jesus and Paul raise the crucial question, What is best in life and how do we experience it? Both answer the question rather ironically: If we want to live—*really* live—then we must deny our own selfish desires and focus on making others happy. In so doing, we will experience a life of true joy and deep contentment that can never come about by living primarily to gratify ourselves. From this perspective, the attractively packaged sexual adventurism displayed all around us as desirable is in reality brutish and dehumanizing. We would be wrong, however, to say that the biblical authors we have studied were ascetic about sex and pleasure. It would be foreign to their thinking to say that God delights in miserable and unfulfilled people. Proverbs in particular espouses the viewpoint that the greatest happiness comes as a direct result of living in harmony with the order that God created. Applied to the realm of human sexuality, this means that those who enjoy sex the most are faithful married couples who take great delight in fulfilling each other.

Ironically, many of the "heroes" of modern books, movies, television, and so on are portrayed as experts at manipulating other people to

gain what they want from them. Sadly enough, the number of authors and directors using these same media forms to make excellent social commentaries is in the minority. Sexual encounters, even in the dramas of real life, are often placed on the same casual level as enjoying a good meal (cf. Prov. 30:20). This mentality has not increased the ability of rational human beings to realize their full potential but has rather had a debilitating effect! Sex is best when it is part of a total relationship in which two people love and desire to please each other and each feels secure and unafraid of rejection if he or she fails to "perform" superbly in bed. Permanence and security in the relationship are major factors in sexual contentment.

Life lived on the level of manipulation is in actuality subhuman, a cheap imitation of real life. The idea of two people *using* each other to satisfy their physical appetites would be repugnant to Jesus and the Apostle Paul. They would assert that selfish living is truncated living, that pleasure gained through using others is only a pitiful shadow of the real joy involved in giving yourself unselfishly for another and happily receiving back what that person gives to you. This is not at all to diminish sexual desire or pleasure but to put them in their rightful place.

Sex should be an enjoyable part of married life, and husbands and wives would do well to adopt the lighthearted fantasy of the Song of Songs. This is true although there are few men who could say honestly that their wives are the most beautiful women in the country and few women who could say their husbands are the most handsome men around (cf. Song 1:8; 2:2–3; 5:10, and so forth). And even those few who are exceptionally beautiful or handsome will grow old and wrinkled. Yet each husband or wife can affirm the great worth of his or her mate and experience tremendous satisfaction in loving that person. On the honeymoon there will be the joy of discovery and the considerable intensity of lovemaking, as expressed in Song of Songs 4:9–5:1. As the couple becomes more experienced, their pleasure will probably increase, although the frequency of their lovemaking diminishes. They will have pleasures both new and old, just like the couple in the Song 7:1–13. Each era of the marriage will hold its own joys if the husband

and wife know how to grow old together in the security of knowing that their relationship is built on far more than physical appearance. Sex is an important part of marriage, but it is only one aspect of a multidimensional relationship. If the total relationship is not good, the meaning and pleasure of sex will disintegrate. Conversely, all through life a marriage based upon unselfish love can produce the kind of joy that inspires poetry—poetry like that found in the Song.

If, however, you are single and frustrated with your status, or are contentedly single yet desiring marriage at some future time, the challenge is to make wise decisions now that will lead to the most joy when you do marry. Try to imagine now what would make a lifetime with another person the best and determine to live wisely, making a conscious effort to become the kind of person whom another would love to have as a marriage partner. Avoid immediate gratification of desire that would in any way spoil your marriage. Like a beautiful flower bud, wait for the springlike warmth of your wedding night before you blossom; and then enjoy all the delights of your husband or wife in the security of your own garden as did the happy couple in the Song 4:9–5:1. Having a good flower garden is worth the time and effort needed to bring it to full blossom.

Note

1. W. Hugh Missildine, *Your Inner Child of the Past* (New York: Simon and Schuster, 1963), p. 297. Missildine's chapter entitled "Sexual Stimulation" offers an excellent analysis of the problems created by our culture's overemphasis on sex. See especially pp. 295–301.

Index

Aaron, 15
Abstinence, 126, 127
Achaicus, 107
Achilles, 158, 160
Adultery:
  Deuteronomy on, 19, 22–23
  Jesus' teaching on, 85
  Proverbs on, 38, 42–49
Aeschines, 158
Afterlife, 12, 39
Akiba, Rabbi, 61, 88–89, 90
Amores 53 (Lucian), 159–60
Apocalyptism, 132
Apocrypha, 69, 88
Apostasy, 16, 17
Aristophanes, 118–19, 158
Asceticism, 109–11, 136
Athenaeus, 117

Babylonian mythology, 39
Beauty, praise of, 56–57, 63–72, 78, 171
Beastiality, 25
Betrothal, 98–99
Birth control, 12, 170

Bisexuality, 155
Bride price, 2, 21, 22, 169

Canaanites, 14
Castration, 24
Celibacy:
  1 Corinthians on, 99–100, 124–29,
    136, 174
  Jesus' teaching on, 97–100
1 Chronicles, 23–24
Cicero, 112
1 Corinthians, 104–40
  celibacy, 99–100, 124–29, 136, 174
  Christian sexual ethics versus Greek cul-
    tural norms, 114–21
  on divorce, 95, 129–31
  on engaged couples, 131–35
  on incest, 111–14
  interpretation of, 104–7
  libertines versus asceticism, 110–11,
    124–25
  on marriage relationship, 124–36, 175
  on prostitution, 121–24
Covenants/treaties, 9–11, 16–17
Cultic prostitution, 23

Dead Sea Scrolls, 99
Deipnosophistae (Atheneus), 117
Deuteronomy, 2–3, 5, 8–27, 168, 169
    on adultery, 19, 22–23
    ancient Hebrew culture, 8–11
    on bestiality, 25
    compared to Proverbs, 30–31, 35, 49
    on divorce, 2, 17–20, 90, 94
    on incest, 25, 112
    on interracial marriage, 14–16
    on marriage relationships, 11–13
    on polygamy, 13–14, 17
    on premarital sex, 20–22
    on prostitution, 23–24
    on rape, 2–3, 20, 22, 169
    on transvestism, 24
Dio Chrysostom, 116
Divorce, 5
    1 Corinthians on, 95, 129–31
    Deuteronomy on, 2, 17–20, 90, 94
    Jesus' teaching on, 84, 90–97, 129–30,
        173–74
    Malachi on, 38
Downtrodden, Jesus concern for, 86–88
Driver, S. R., 21

Ecclesiastes, 61
Egyptian love poetry, 62–63, 64, 67–68,
    76, 78–79
Engaged couples, 131–35
1 Enoch, 145
Epictetus, 160–61
Essenes, 99
Exodus, 15, 22, 25

Facial laceration, 14
Fortunatus, 107

Genesis, 13, 17, 25, 70–71, 94, 98,
    100, 123, 147–48, 163
Gittin, 90
Gomorrah, 149
Greeks (ancient):
    acceptance of homosexuality, 154–62
    cultural norms, 114–21
    women, 116–18

Hebrew Wisdom tradition (*see*
    Proverbs)
Hetairai, 116–17, 155
Hillel, Rabbi, 88, 90, 126
Homer, 158
Homosexuality, 24, 118, 141–66
    Greco-Roman acceptance of, 154–62
    Jewish abhorrence of, 147–50
    Philo on, 150–54
Horace, 119
Humor in Song of Songs, 76–79

Idolatry, 144–47, 149–50
Incest, 25, 111–14
Inheritance, 17, 169
"Instruction of Amenemope, The," 31
Interracial marriage, 14–16
Isaiah, 24

Jacob, 17
Jeremiah, 15
Jesus, teachings of, 84–102, 172
    adultery, 85
    celibacy, 97–100, 174
    concern for downtrodden, 86–88
    divorce, 84, 90–97, 129–30, 173–74
    prostitution, 88–89
    purity of thoughts, 87–88
Jewish Sibylline Oracles, 148–49
Judges, 15
Judith, 69
Juvenal, 119–20

Kethuboth, 96, 130
Kidner, Derek, 45
1 Kings, 16

Leah, 17
Lesbianism, 162
Levirate marriage, 12–13
Leviticus, 24, 25, 112, 147
Libertines, 110–13, 115, 121–24, 136
Lucian, 159–60, 162
Luke, 93, 95–96

Malachi, 38
Mark, 18, 91–96, 99, 132, 145, 174
Marriage alliances, 16–17
Marriage relationship:
    1 Corinthians on, 124–36, 175
    Deuteronomy on, 11–13
    Proverbs on, 48
Martial, 162
Mary, 99
Matthew, 18, 85–86, 88–100, 145
McKane, W., 41
Media, 171, 175–76
Memorabilia (Xenophon), 158
Miriam, 15
Misnah, 90, 95–96, 99, 112, 126, 130
Mistresses, 116–i7, 155
Moses, 10, 15
Mourning, 14

New Testament:
1 Corinthians (*see* 1 Corinthians)
    Luke, 93, 95–96
    Mark, 18, 91–96, 99, 132, 145, 174
    Matthew, 18, 85–86, 88–100, 145
    Revelation, 60, 132, 145
    Romans, 142–46, 148, 149, 158–64
    (*see also* Jesus, teachings of)
Numbers, 14–15, 25

Odes (Horace), 119
Old Testament:
    Apocrypha, 69, 88
    1 Chronicles, 23–24
    Deuteronomy (*see* Deuteronomy)
    Ecclesiastes, 61
    Exodus, 15, 22, 25
    Genesis, 13, 17, 25, 70–71, 94, 98,
        100, 123, 147–48, 163
    Isaiah, 24
    Jeremiah, 15
    Judges, 15
    1 Kings, 16
    Leviticus, 24, 25, 112, 147
    Malachi, 38
    Numbers, 14–15, 25

Proverbs (*see* Proverbs)
    Psalms, 24
    2 Samuel, 15
    Song of Songs (*see* Song of Songs)
On Abraham (Philo), 151

Patroclus, 158, 160
Paul, 95, 96
    (*see also* 1 Corinthians; Romans)
Pentateuch, 25
Petronius, 119
Philo of Alexandria, 150–54
Plato, 155–57
Plutarch, 161
Polygamy, 13–14, 17
Pope, Marvin, 60, 69
Premarital sex, Deuteronomy on, 20–22
Prostitution, 117–18
    1 Corinthians on, 121–24
    Deuteronomy on, 23–24
    Jesus' teaching on, 88–89
    Proverbs on, 48–49
Protagorus (Plato), 157
Proverbs, 5, 30–52, 125, 169–70, 173,
    175
    compared to Deuteronomy, 30–31, 35,
        49
    on fidelity, 40–42
    on prostitution, 48–49
    Wisdom School, 35–37, 47, 50, 169,
        170
Purity of thoughts, 87

Rabbinic writings, 88–90, 95–96, 98,
    99, 112, 126
Rachel, 17
Rape, Deuteronomy on, 2–3, 20, 22, 169
Ras Shamra texts, 14
Remarriage, 19, 20, 135
Revelation, 60, 132, 145
Romans, 142–46, 148, 149, 158–64
Roman Sibylline Oracles, 148

Saggs, H. W. F., 24
Samuel, 15

Sanhedrin, 15
Satyricon (Petronius), 119
Seduction, 45–48, 170, 173
Septuagint, 15, 61
Sermon on the Mount, 85, 93
Shammai, 90, 96, 126
Sheol, 39
Sibylline Oracles, 148–49
Sirach, 41, 87
"Sixth Satire" (Juvenal), 119–20
Slavonic Enoch, 149
Socrates, 157–59
Sodom, 147–48, 151 152
Song of Songs (Song of Solomon), 5,
    53–81, 176, 177
    allegorical interpretation of, 60–61
    Egyptian love poetry and, 62–63, 64,
    67–68, 76, 78–79
    humor in, 76–79
    praise of beauty, 56–57, 63–72, 78
    virginity, 72–76
Stephanas, 107
Stoning, 11, 21, 23
Strabo, 118
Swain, Lionel, 133
Symposium, (Plato), 155–56

Temple prostitutes, 118, 121, 124
Ten Commandments, 10
Testament of Issachar, 87
Testament of Levi, 147
Testament of Naphtali, 126
Testaments of the Twelve Patriachs, 147
Timarchus, 158–59
Tobit, 88
Transvestism, Deuteronomy on, 24

Venereal disease, 40
Virginity, 11–12, 20–22
    Song of Songs on, 72–76

White, John B., 62
Widows, 129, 135
Wisdom of Solomon, 149–50
Wisdom School, 35–37, 47, 50, 169, 170
Woes of the Messiah, 132

Xenophon, 157–59

Yahweh, 10
Yebamoth, 99, 130

Zipporah, 15

WESTMAR COLLEGE LIBRARY

WESTMAR COLLEGE LIBRARY

W9-BOA-102